Leading a Pastoral Team

Approaches to pastoral middle management

Leading a Pastoral Team

Approaches to pastoral middle management

Les Bell and Peter Maher

BASIL BLACKWELL

For Georgina, Steven and Sarah

First published 1986

© Les Bell and Peter Maher 1986

Published by Basil Blackwell Ltd
108 Cowley Road
Oxford OX4 1JF
England

British Library Cataloguing in Publication Data
Bell, Les
   Leading a pastoral team.
   1. School social work—Management
   I. Title   II. Maher, Peter
   371.4'6   LB3013.4

ISBN 0-631-14211-8

Typeset in 11 on 13pt Plantin
by Katerprint Typesetting Services Ltd, Oxford
Printed in Great Britain

Contents

1 The development of pastoral organisation

Introduction

This book is about the delivery of pastoral care within schools and about the ways in which that delivery is managed. It does not seek to present an academic analysis of the current situation in schools or of how the range of different types of pastoral provision which can be identified in schools has developed. Nor does it set out to provide a critique of the various approaches to pastoral care, although it does acknowledge that various approaches exist which have to be taken into account by those who seek to manage pastoral care in schools.

The book starts from the assumption that those most closely involved with the day-to-day organisation of pastoral care are the pastoral middle-managers, the heads of house or heads of year. It is written primarily for them and for those who aspire to those positions. Their main concern will be to make the system in which they find themselves work as effectively as possible rather than to change it, since, in most cases, pastoral middle-managers are rarely in a position to bring about significant, large-scale organisational changes. In order to be a successful and effective head of house or year, it is first necessary for the pastoral middle-manager to understand the context within which s/he has to work, and then to be able to adopt and adapt approaches which suit his or her own situation. Only those approaches which are appropriate to a given situation can work, therefore we offer a topography of pastoral care within which pastoral middle-managers can locate themselves and their pastoral organisation.

Although we recognise the importance of relating activity to situation, we also argue that it is possible to identify a series of practical managerial skills which can be adapted and used by the pastoral middle-manager in his/her own situation provided that s/he understands the essential elements of that situation. We argue throughout the book that an understanding of the context is crucial, especially in the areas of using tutorial time and developing pastoral activity, if the pastoral middle-manager is to avoid the pitfalls inherent in any attempt to use 'off the shelf' solutions to specific problems. Our approach is based on the assumption that s/he will undertake this analysis of his/her own situation; hence the lack of academic analysis of pastoral structures in this book. What has to be analysed is the particular school and the way in which the pastoral provision within that school is organised.

To carry out such an analysis, the pastoral middle-manager has to be aware of a number of significant developments in the area of pastoral care. Chapter 1 deals with these and places the growth of pastoral care in an historical perspective, so that the individual can recognise some of the general elements of this growth as they might be evident in his/her own school, perhaps in conflicting or contradictory ways, for instance, by examining what the school tells parents, teachers and pupils about its pastoral provision. We point out, in Chapter 2, that these messages are sometimes less than clear and can confuse even those who are responsible for managing the pastoral system in the school. We do not aim to provide a detailed guide to the complex topic of the development of pastoral care and therefore there is a short bibliography at the end of each chapter with references which extend and develop points made in the chapter, and sources which offer different analyses or approaches. Thus, the reader can explore and extend the argument developed in the text and also compare that argument with alternative approaches as s/he considers the various strategies available to the pastoral middle-manager.

The role of the pastoral middle-manager has two essential elements. The first is the need to establish and develop the pastoral team of house or year tutors for whom the head of house or year has direct responsibility. This team has to be managed rather than left to its own devices if the pastoral system is to work effectively in any school. Chapters 3 and 4 deal extensively with the development and management of the pastoral team by the pastoral middle-manager. Team development has to be deliberately managed and needs to be based on an open approach to establishing priorities and responsibilities as well as on a concern for those factors which encourage active and supportive team membership, such as effective communication and well organised meetings. At the end of these chapters (and of most of the other chapters) is a series of exercises which can be used by the pastoral team leader to adapt our ideas to his/her situation in order to gain some practical benefit by trying out the processes identified here in his/her own context.

The second essential element of the role of the pastoral middle-manager, is co-ordinating the pastoral activities of the team. Chapter 5, in considering how the role of the form tutor might be developed by the team leader, begins to examine this. The ways in which the activities of individual form tutors have to be combined and co-ordinated in order to blend into an effective, team-based approach to pastoral activity, require an understanding on the part of the pastoral middle-manager of how the concerns felt by the form tutors affect what form tutors actually do as seen by the form tutors themselves. By taking this as a starting point the team leader can establish what is being done, what can be done more effectively, and what still needs to be done. This assessment may lead the pastoral middle-manager to want to change some of what the team does or to alter the current method of doing things.

Chapter 6 provides an outline approach to managing change within the team. Most changes may best be carried through by recognising that resistance to change will always exist, but that it can be minimised by inviting colleagues to participate in the change process rather than by excluding them from it. It offers a model of change management which can be adapted to most situations.

This is followed, in Chapter 7, by a discussion of pastoral activity, where we extend those ideas touched upon in Chapter 5 and suggest that pastoral middle-managers should take responsibility for developing their own tutorial programme which they can manage in the way most appropriate to their own situation. We conclude that, in order to manage a pastoral team effectively, the pastoral team leader's approach must be firmly located in his/her own situation rather than based on an analysis of situations which only approximate to it. In order to help the leader to understand his/her own situation, we now turn to a brief consideration of how pastoral care has developed and how those developments might have affected the pastoral organisation in individual schools.

The context: schools and their management

The nature of pastoral care in schools, the structures created to deliver pastoral care in schools, the relationships which are involved in this delivery, and the activities which are recognised as appropriate to pastoral care, have all changed significantly over the last twenty years.

It is important for the pastoral team manager to understand the development of various forms of pastoral organisation and the historical context within which those developments took place. If the pastoral team leader is to aid the team's effective working within the climate of the school, s/he needs to understand the extent to which the pastoral work is determined by the wider school organisation, and to be able to recognise the tensions operating there..

There have been significant changes in school management over a period which coincides with that during which pastoral care has emerged as a significant feature of school life. The trend, particularly in the 1960s and early 1970s, was towards larger schools. Prior to that, in a small school environment, a relatively autocratic style of leadership was expected from secondary headteachers. With one deputy and a teaching staff of about twenty, this was an environment where such an autocratic approach could flourish, was felt to be appropriate and was largely unchallenged. Such a style, however, was less suitable as the size of schools increased. Expansion was partly due to the growth of the post-war pupil population and partly to the amalgamation of schools which took place when local education authorities carried out their policies of comprehensive reorganisation. The resulting institutions brought with them a number of significant features which inevitably affected the way in which they were managed. In many cases, those appointed to posts at all levels in the reorganised schools had carried considerable responsibility in a smaller school, prior to reorganisation.

It was not unusual for the newly-appointed deputy headteachers in a reorganised comprehensive school to have previously been headteachers in their own right. Clearly, this would affect the way the headteacher felt able to manage the school. Moreover, the scale of the task of headship changed. While it was perfectly possible to see how a headteacher might play a solo, autocratic role in a small school, such a position was much more difficult in a larger institution. An obvious solution was to delegate responsibility to other members of staff, but this raised problems. First, there was the question of the working relationship between the headteacher and the staff to whom responsibility for some aspect of the school's organisation had been delegated. Second, implicit in this style of organisation was a change in the promotional routes for teachers. These factors were to have a significant influence on the management role of the headteacher.

The senior management teams of comprehensive schools often looked for a way to partition different aspects of the management task.

One such method of partition was to offer two deputy headteachers responsibility for the distinct areas of 'academic' and 'pastoral' elements of the school's work. That is not to say that those two areas were properly understood; indeed, it was symptomatic of the paucity of thinking at the time that headteachers found themselves at a loss when they had three deputy headteachers of equivalent status. Having established one as 'Curriculum Deputy' and another as 'Pastoral Deputy', what was the third to do? It is enlightening to read the job specifications of some of these 'Senior Master/Mistress – Deputy Head Scale' posts. Often the description was as mundane as 'responsible for arranging flowers in the foyer, liaising with the PTA, and senior girls' welfare'.

With much of the responsibility of the senior management delegated in this way, it was important that the management team operated effectively; there must be some doubt that such groups do operate effectively and there is a need for research in this area. The way in which the tasks are partitioned could well mitigate against their functioning properly. It is certainly the case, we would argue, that such a division of labour affects the perception of other teachers of the relative importance of different elements of the school's function.

Here was the start of a hierarchical approach to management tasks within the school which was to become the norm. Senior management teams appeared, to many of the rest of the staff, to set themselves apart, meeting in private enclave, to discuss issues of policy. No matter how impassioned the pleas of the senior management team that their time was spent in debating the trivia rather than engaging in high-powered decision-making, other staff were simply not prepared to accept it. Such a perception was compounded when the senior management team, or the headteacher at least, had the power to promote an individual's career. The management team appeared to have both the power of information and the power of benefaction. Part of the difficulty that now faces the middle-manager is persuading the team that it has an effective role. The temptation to play upon an 'us and them' mentality as an excuse for inactivity is very strong indeed and one of the tensions to which the middle-manager must be alert.

The second phase in the approach to the management of the larger schools came in the approach to the middle-order rank of management. It was an inevitable solution to further subdivide the tasks that had been delegated to particular deputy headteachers. In the vast majority of cases, schools chose to subdivide their academic function through departments or faculties. There have been attempts to look for 'linkages' between these areas of interest but, largely, those initially devised structures have remained unchallenged. Often there was fierce competition for these posts of responsibility. Where several schools were amalgamating to form a single comprehensive, it was often the head of department in the academic grammar school who became head of department in the comprehensive. There was thus an important issue of status prevalent at the time, that continues to dominate our attitudes to the role of middle-managers. The academic departments received the accolade of high-status tasks; almost inevitably, any role offered to the unsuccessful applicant was bound to take on the mantle of a low-status area.

The perceived difficulty of the large school was that of size. It was certainly the case that in a small school of only a few hundred children, most students (and their parents) could expect to know and be known by the vast majority of teachers. Where the numbers of pupils doubled, trebled, or indeed expanded, almost beyond belief, the anxiety for the individual pupil became acute. Much emphasis was placed upon the need to ensure that each child was known to at least one teacher who was to take responsibility for its welfare. Thus, the system of institutionalised care and the conventional wisdom of the pastoral system as it is known in the modern comprehensive school was born.

Pastoral care as control

In appointing staff to take a lead in this defined function of care, the logic was followed that those who had dealt with the 'less intelligent' or the 'less highly motivated', were best placed to carry out this role. It is worth noting that from the outset the perception of pastoral care was of a primitive, problem-centred activity to do with pupils of low ability and poor motivation. Those appointed to middle-management tasks in comprehensive schools were often the 'failures' in the promotion race for the academic posts. Immediately, then, pastoral care was to do with 'less able', 'poorly motivated' pupils and was 'low status'.

The rationale behind the setting up of such primitive formal pastoral care systems is much the same as that which underlies the departmental or faculty structure; it is a truism of educational management that each element of the school's task, once identified, has, in some way, to be 'institutionalised', to ensure that the task is carried out. Thus, if the headteacher wishes to demonstrate that the school is properly undertaking the caring element of its role, it is necessary to point to the particular part of the organisation whose prime task is to carry out that care. A similar logic supports the establishment of English and mathematics departments. Formal recognition within the structure is required to offer a particular activity proper status. The institutionalised caring function had, from its outset, a second-class status.

The way that schools chose to institutionalise their various functions can, in retrospect, be seen to have created a number of difficulties. For example, assumptions that mathematics was the exclusive province of the mathematics department, and English was taught by English teachers were eventually challenged by Bullock and Cockcroft. Similarly, the fact that, on paper at least, certain teachers were actually paid to be pastoral, created the illusion in some quarters that pastoral care was carried out only by pastoral teachers. It was recognised that all teachers had some pastoral role, but it was also felt that some were more pastoral than others.

Partly, the problem was the response to the pastoral hierarchy; the structures set up to ensure the consistency of care were led by heads of house, heads of year, heads of school and so on. The understanding of those roles has only developed with time. It is certainly the case that in the early days, in the first generation of formal pastoral care, these pastoral middle-managers were seen as super disciplinarians. Often their responsibility began and ended with discipline. They were the authority to whom others with discipline problems were to turn for help. They were rarely seen as team leaders and, though grudgingly admired by some staff, they were essentially regarded as second-class teachers because they did not have a strong subject base.

There was a sense in which these early pastoral systems reflected a level of philosophical thought. The different types of system established were a response to differently perceived aspects of the care that was to be offered. The house system, very much a reflection of the private sector of education, tried to put the emphasis on consistency of contact between families and school. This vertical grouping of students, perhaps representing a quarter of a school, was overseen by a head of house, who would follow through the house class group from year 1 to years 5 or 6. Where possible, siblings would join the same vertical grouping; contact for parents was then minimised to a few well-known teachers. The emphasis of the vertical group structure was very much upon care and consistency.

The horizontal grouping would often partition the student population by year group. In some cases, clusters of year groups would form 'schools within schools'. Here the emphasis was much more upon administrative convenience. Many of the things that the school wanted to do *to* the pupil were focused upon year groups. Particular curricular stages were year group centred, areas of guidance were year group centred, contact with parents through reports and parent evenings were year group centred. Such a year group centred division seemed sensible. There were problems of continuity that were offered by vertical house grouping. Attempts to overcome this through the device of 'rolling year tutors' and so on are still in evidence today.

For those who wanted the overt care of the vertical system combined with the administrative convenience of the horizontal system, the 'matrix' combined the two, often specifying that those staff with vertical responsibility were to do with care, whilst those concerned with horizontal responsibility were to do with administrative tasks. An analysis of a school with such an overkill approach to pastoral care is minutely dissected in *Education and Care* (Best *et al*, 1983).

Each of these systems was in some way or another a response to the perceived needs of the caring and control functions of the school. They shared, too, the common element of subdividing the large school population, so overcoming some of the criticism of the large comprehensive. Even so, it was clear that any one person, super disciplinarian though they might be, was unable to carry this task alone. Even in the very early days of institutionalised care, the emphasis was upon the role of the form tutor. It says much that we are still struggling with the problem.

Pastoral care as individual need
If the first generation of pastoral care was concerned mainly with the need to control and discipline large numbers of pupils and to enable them to feel that they had a place within a large organisation, the second became overlaid with another set of functions which had more to do with specific individual needs. It had, as its central feature, care based on individual counselling from the pastoral middle-manager, the head of house or head of year. This was also offered, in theory at least, by the form tutor.

It was during this second phase in the development of pastoral care that much of the work on individual counselling developed. Individual care, the logic went, meant devoting time and attention to individual students. Clearly, this required special skill on the part of the teacher, and since the majority of a school's staff were, in fact, form tutors, it followed that most teachers were expected to have this expertise. Even where they did possess the skills, individual counselling demanded a lot of time, the one commodity that is in short supply in schools. It meant that the form tutor must find some activity to keep the rest of the tutees involved while one individual was being counselled. It was understandable, therefore, that the form or registration period became widely identified as a suitable time for this activity.

Pastoral care as group activity

The third generation of pastoral care appears to have developed in response to the problems with which many tutors found themselves confronted as they attempted to deal with individuals in group situations. It was far more difficult to counsel one individual, expecting that the rest of the pupil group could find some more or less worthwhile activity while the individual counselling was taking place, than it was to explore the possibility of counselling groups rather than individuals. Therefore, what had begun as an individually based activity started to change into a group activity. The form group became the basis for counselling. Much of the success or otherwise of this activity depended on the form tutor's ability to operate within the very real constraints of the situation, which imposed severe time and space limits upon what could be achieved or even attempted and which relied heavily on the tutor's capability to develop suitable strategies to enable individual caring to take place within a larger group situation.

Some year and form tutors could operate successfully within these constraints. They recognised that the situation demanded the provision of valid activities within the tutorial framework. For many others, however, the change in emphasis from individual to group-based work raised the difficult issue of what to do with the form tutor periods. One common response in local education authorities as a whole as well as in individual schools, was to buy instant solutions such as Active Tutorial Work. This response has been tried in other areas of education. Sometimes it has worked and sometimes it has not. The significant factors in determining the extent to which such bought-in solutions as ATW work in any school appear to be the amount of time devoted to training the staff in using the material, so that they understand what is and is not possible with it. All too often, however, ATW and similar schemes have been introduced to support tutor group activity without any reference to tutors' abilities to work within a group tutoring framework and without developing, on the part of tutors, a thorough understanding of how such approaches work, what particular skills are necessary, and what forms of tutor-pupil relationships have to be established in order for these approaches to be successful.

The pastoral curriculum

The development of pastoral care as a group-based activity tended to take place in isolation from the rest of the curriculum and, indeed, the adoption of some group programmes reinforced the separateness of pastoral activity from the rest of the activities of the school. The fourth generation of pastoral development, 'the pastoral curriculum', can best be understood as a deliberate attempt to break down this artificial isolation of caring from the rest of school life. Marland (1980), in first describing the term, was most careful in detailing his definition of it. For Marland, the pastoral curriculum was merely a sub-set of the whole school curriculum. It was that part of the curriculum which, more or less, dealt with the development of the whole person. The activity which was carried out during the form tutor period was a subset of the pastoral curriculum. Thus, by Marland's definition, the pastoral curriculum was in no sense subsumed in tutorial activity. There were some elements of the pastoral curriculum which were best approached through the medium of the tutorial group-based work. There were, however, some elements of work which, quite properly, should be conducted by specialist teachers in their subject areas.

Let us take, for example, the topic of health education. Some elements of this subject might be covered by a form tutor as part of a tutorial programme. Other elements might be covered by the science department during compulsory science lessons in years 1, 2 and 3. Careers education might properly be dealt with by specialist careers staff when dealing with post-16 provision in the fifth year; but some earlier specific advice would be needed about implications for future careers in relation to subject option choices for fourth and fifth year study. It would be appropriate for any specialist teacher, even at first-year level, when introducing pupils to their specialist fields, to talk about possible career options associated with success in that subject.

Thus, from Marland's standpoint, the concept of the pastoral curriculum is a very broad one indeed. It is certainly an issue that schools need to take up. It is important to ascertain how well the term and its implications are understood, not only by a minority of teachers with specific pastoral responsibility, but by the staff as a whole. It is certainly important that the senior management team understand the use of the term. If theirs is the role of initiating and co-ordinating discussion on curricular issues, the development of the pastoral curriculum will certainly be enhanced or limited by their level of appreciation. The form tutor, too, needs to understand the nature and validity of that element of the pastoral curriculum which is to be contained within a tutorial programme. We discuss the crucial role of the form tutor in Chapter 5 and pastoral activity in Chapter 7.

Most important here is the discussion of curricular issues in relation to pastoral care. For those who saw pastoral care as an emergency first-aid system to deal with discipline problems, Marland's introduction of the term pastoral curriculum is certainly a quantum-leap. Implicit in the term are two tensions which need to be discussed and resolved within the school. The first, as we have already indicated, is the process of curriculum planning. How does the school set about developing policies which ensure that the curriculum is properly planned and that the experiences which the school determines are appropriate for its students are adequately covered? The second tension may mark the development of another stage in the evolution of pastoral care. Associated with the teaching of certain elements of the pastoral curriculum is the question of the appropriate teaching style. Some topics do not lend themselves to the didactic style of classroom teaching. Many teachers have found themselves confronted with the need to re-evaluate their teaching approach in such settings. Some would argue that this re-evaluation of teaching method, has, in turn, led to a reappraisal of teaching methods employed elsewhere in the formal curriculum. Such a radical review of teaching process has led to marked changes in classroom organisation and in the learning experiences of the students.

The problem facing many pastoral middle-managers is coping with a primitive view of pastoral care exhibited by other staff, not least perhaps by members of the senior management team. If the head of year or house is perceived to be the person responsible for maintaining (other peoples') discipline in the school, it is difficult for him/her to emerge from under a welter of paper, queues of children and, usually, a considerable teaching load, to devote time to developing another, more constructive role. Even where this is not the case, it is possible that the pastoral middle-manager will be confronted by a range of conflicting assumptions about pastoral care which derive from perspectives which s/he may not share and which s/he may no longer recognise as being relevant to his/her understanding of the pastoral structure of the school. Such perceptions may, however, have a significant effect on the attitude of colleagues towards pastoral care in the school and towards its manager.

The middle-manager may also be confronted by members of his/her team who are demotivated. There are some teachers, who, having developed professionally in a climate where the primitive definition of pastoral care pertained, view the pastoral team leader's role as limited. With this view of pastoral care, it is probable that such teachers consider their time with their form group as, essentially, a waste of time. It is unlikely that they understand what is meant by the term pastoral curriculum, or that they understand their role within a tutorial programme. Could you imagine a head of department operating in a situation where members of the departmental staff held such views about their subject? What would the department head do if a teacher expressed such negative views about the department's activity? How much more absurd would the situation be if these views, if not shared by the senior management team, gained a level of sympathy from that quarter?

Such an attitude towards pastoral care presents pastoral middle-managers with a number of problems. How do they offer effective leadership to their team, some of whom may be demotivated? How do they motivate their form tutors generally, and the less highly motivated form tutor specifically? How do they operate in a school where their work may not be properly understood? How do they effect a change in attitudes towards pastoral care within the school? These questions need to be posed and answered.

This book seeks to address those issues. It assumes that the pastoral structure within which most pastoral middle-managers work will contain elements of all four generations of pastoral care and that various members of the pastoral team may, at least initially, subscribe to different elements of those generations. In view of this, the pastoral middle-manager will need to have a proactive rather than a reactive role, that is, the pastoral team will require to be actively managed as a unit rather than allowed to exist as a group of individuals. To review the pastoral curriculum with pastoral tutors or others who may still be operating with perceptions of pastoral work derived from notions of control will require, on the part of the pastoral middle-manager, the abilities to manage a team and to bring about effective change. These activities will be discussed in Chapters 3, 4 and 7. All those elements which combine to make up the pastoral work of any school will, irrespective of the generation of pastoral care from which they are derived, be formed into a more or less coherent approach to caring in its various aspects by the pastoral philosophy of the school. It is this philosophy which provides the framework of values and attitudes from which pastoral activity takes its meaning in any school. It is to a discussion of the philosophy of pastoral care that we now turn.

Exercises

1 Compare the pastoral organisation of your own school with the three stages of development of pastoral organisation presented in this chapter. Can you identify elements of each in your own school? Which model predominates? Does this change over time?
2 Examine the attitudes of colleagues who consult you in your capacity as pastoral middle-manager. What is their perception of your role?
3 Examine the perceptions of your pastoral team members about the pastoral provision in your school. Do they have a shared view of the pastoral system? Which of the four models in this chapter is the one which most closely approximates to the majority view of your colleagues?
4 What is your view of your role as pastoral middle-manager? Does it coincide with the predominant view of the pastoral system held within the school; with the predominant view of colleagues who consult you as a pastoral middle-manager; with the views of members of your pastoral team?

References and further reading

Best, R., Ribbins, P. and Jarvis, C. (eds) 1980: *Perspectives on Pastoral Care*. Heinemann.
Best, R., Ribbins, P., Jarvis, C. and Oddy, D. 1983: *Education and Care*. Heinemann.
Blackburn, K. 1975: *The Tutor*. Heinemann.
Hamblin, D. 1978: *The Teacher and Pastoral Care*. Blackwell.
Marland, M. 1974: *Pastoral Care*. Heinemann.
Marland, M. 1980: 'The Pastoral Curriculum'. In Best *et al.* (eds) *Perspectives on Pastoral Care*. Heinemann.
Vaughan, T. 1975 *Education and the aims of counselling*. Blackwell.

2 The philosophy of caring

Why have a philosophy of caring?

Out of the different perspectives of pastoral care detailed in the previous chapter arise a range of philosophies that underpin the caring process and shape what we do in schools. Indeed different sets of ideas may lead to radically contrasting outcomes. For example, one rationale for a vertical grouping of pupils into a house system could be the principle that there should be a continuity of contact between pupils and the pastoral team and parents and the pastoral team, emphasising the familial model. In contrast, the needs of cohorts of pupils at essentially similar points in their school career leads to an age-based horizontal structure. These sets of ideas or 'philosophies' may affect the decisions that we take, both on a long-term and on a day-to-day basis, and will determine which decisions are regarded as important.

Many of the decisions that we take daily in a secondary school context may well have profound implications for our students. An obvious example is examination entry policy. Having decided that a student is best suited to one type of examination, to what extent do we allow the student or parents to alter that decision? Clearly, we could argue that our professional assessment, based on many years' experience, has the good of the child at heart; to concede to the parental or student wishes would only jeopardise the student's likelihood of success. In certain contexts, the parents could well view our decision as wrong.

A second example might be our policy towards options selection for fourth and fifth year courses. How limiting will the structure of our option groupings be? Do we offer a free choice of all the option subjects available and then construct our timetable around the declared interests of the students? Do we make some subjects or groups of subjects compulsory? Clearly, the way that we approach this task has far-reaching effects upon the future of the students that we serve.

The decision-making process that accompanies policy formation, which then may dictate the answers to these and other questions, has several different roots. The following examples may be caricatures; none the less it may be possible to recognise your school amongst them.

In the hand-to-mouth decision-making process the head or senior management team react to a given set of circumstances in haste and announce a policy which, more often than not, is ill considered and survives for only a limited period of time. In such a management environment it would not be unknown for a 'decision' to be announced at morning break, only to be revised by lunchtime on the same day.

Some headteachers who adopt a far more egalitarian approach to school management might want to involve staff as fully as possible in the decision-making process. A matter of possible policy would be referred to the staff, or to a committee representing staff opinion, so that the matter could be discussed fully. The views of the staff would then be considered when decisions on that policy issue were taken, or, in some circumstances, the head might allow the decision to be made by the staff.

What is in evidence in all decision-making processes is the managerial philosophy of the headteacher. Philosophy is perhaps too grand a word to apply to the headteacher who operates on a hand-to-mouth basis; but others will determine their style of managerial approach according to some quite precise, implicit or explicit, philosophy. Many of the most successful headteachers operate on such a philosophical basis and may, indeed, be working within a number of complementary philosophical frameworks.

The effect of managing a school within a philosophical framework is to bring a sense of cohesion and purpose. That philosophy, when it is fully and properly understood by those involved with the school, offers insights into day-to-day practice. Often, when situations arise which need some reference to policy to find a solution, because that policy is philosophically based, the outcome is almost predetermined. Take, for example, the examination entry problem mentioned earlier. A school following the philosophy that 'school knows best' will insist that the school's decision is implemented. On the other hand, a school adopting the philosophy that 'parental rights are paramount' may try to argue their case for a particular type of examination entry but in the end may concede to the parents' wishes.

Philosophy and organisation

It is seldom easy to determine whether a school has adopted a philosophical approach or not without first-hand experience of how the
school operates in practice. The usual way that schools promulgate
their adopted philosophy is through statements of policy often found
in handbooks for staff, parents or pupils. Be warned, though. The
statement of the school's philosophy may not be reflected in practice.
It is possible to find contradictions within such statements.

We can use as illustration the opening two paragraphs of the section
on *Social and pastoral organisation* from the staff handbook of a large
comprehensive school near London. Try to imagine yourself as a new
teacher to this school, perhaps a probationer, who is trying to understand the school's philosophy towards pastoral care:

> 'As comprehensives have developed, discussion of the social and
> pastoral organisation within the schools has revealed widely vary-
> ing views inside the teaching profession. Some, especially in
> deprived areas, see the pastoral work of the staff, and the sub-
> division of the school community, as of major importance to the
> pupils; others would seriously question the need for an organisa-
> tional superstructure to cater for pastoral and social purposes.
>
> Somewhere between these extremes lie the views of many who
> regard sub-division of the school as a necessary and useful admi-
> nistrative device, and recognise the need for extra care inside the
> school for disadvantaged pupils, pupils who have various prob-
> lems often manifested in behavioural difficulties, but who would
> be sceptical of elaborate systems designed to engineer social
> relationships and continuous pastoral care for every pupil.'

How does the teacher, new to the school, view the attitudes towards
pastoral care, having read this statement? There are a number of
messages, both explicit and implicit, in such a statement:

- Pastoral care is most appropriate for 'deprived areas'; there is less
  need, then, for pastoral care in areas that are perceived as 'good'.
- Pastoral care is simply an 'organisational superstructure' and is
  not central to the work of the school.
- Seeing the 'pastoral work of staff . . . as of major importance to
  the pupils' is an extreme view.
- The 'majority view' is that pastoral care is a 'useful administrative device'.
- Pastoral care is needed to help only 'disadvantaged pupils'.

- Pastoral care is to deal with 'problems often manifested in behavioural difficulties'.
- Pastoral care is problem centred and is not meant to provide 'continuous pastoral care for all pupils'.

These, and many more messages are contained in the introduction to the section of the school's staff handbook devoted to the social and pastoral organisation of the school. The impression conveyed is one of disinterest in pastoral care, which clearly takes a secondary role in the task of the school. How does such a statement affect the attitude and motivation of the teacher trying to come to terms with the pastoral element of his/her role?

By contrast, the staff handbook of another large London comprehensive begins the section on pastoral care (called 'Guidance' by this school) with a statement:

> *Purposes of guidance*
> - To support subject teaching, paying attention to the work done by each pupil, assessing progress made and giving encouragement and help.
> - To encourage pupils to play a full part in all school activities.
> - To offer guidance in educational choice-making and career decisions.
> - To help the individual pupil develop values and a sense of toleration and responsibility towards others.
> - To maintain an orderly atmosphere in which all the above is possible.
>
> It follows that these purposes can only be achieved through the interest and commitment of the whole staff. At the same time, our organisation has to be efficient if we are not to overlook the interests of the individual.

The material that follows this introduction offers comprehensive information on a number of related topics. Following a cautionary word about confidentiality there are sections on the role of the form teacher (which is a ten-point job specification); the tutorial period; links with subject teachers; pastoral and departmental record keeping; the form-tutor-based record system, and a section on compiling records for school-leavers.

It is quite possible to suggest that the introductory section of the handbook was an inadequate description of pastoral care or guidance and that the precise details of what was offered subsequently do not represent an exhaustive catalogue of legitimate pastoral care activity.

None the less, a teacher new to this school would have some clear impressions, having read the document, about the espoused position of the school in relation to the guidance offered to the pupils. A teacher in this school would approach the pastoral task safe in the knowledge that his/her role is seen by senior staff as a valuable and legitimate one. Indeed, teachers are encouraged 'to seek early advice from someone in a senior position'.

Philosophy and activity

It is not just in our written statements that we convey to other teachers our attitudes towards pastoral care. Diagrams can be useful to show how the system operates. Figure 1 is a schematic diagram taken from the staff handbook of one of the largest schools in the country. It purports to show 'lines of communication within the pastoral system'. It is squeezed, without explanation, between a brief statement entitled *Form Tutor* and another section headed *Private Study*. Apart from being a very complex statement about lines of communication, the schematic diagram seems to say more than was perhaps intended.

- The only person to hold *all* the information is the director of pastoral care. Is this to say that the pastoral system is run and organised by that person?
- Access to information for the form teachers is very limited. According to the diagram they have no direct contact with the senior management committee, special unit, outside agencies or even their director of pastoral care. This seems to suggest that the form teacher is the least important and valued member of the pastoral team.
- Pastoral care seems to exist separately from any academic organisation.

Clearly, there are many more messages here for the teacher new to the school, not least of which is the relationship between the pastoral aspect of their role and their other responsibilities as a teacher.

The problem of the pastoral/academic dichotomy is spelled out even more clearly in a diagram in another school handbook. This diagram, too, appears in the middle of text with no supporting explanation. It is simply headed *The school structure* (Figure 2). Here, the 'academic' and 'pastoral' elements of the school's activities are shown as being under the separate direction of deputy heads. But there is growing acceptance that, just like English and mathematics teaching, pastoral care

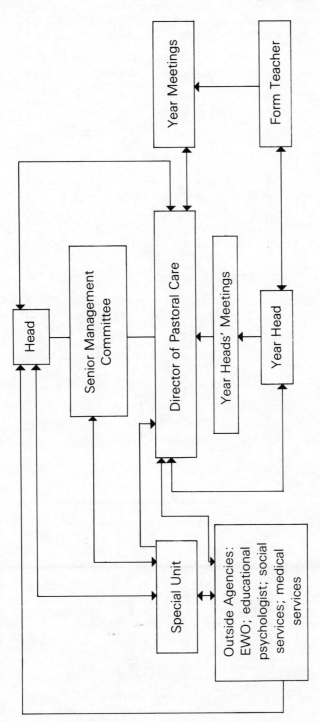

Figure 1: Lines of communication within the pastoral system

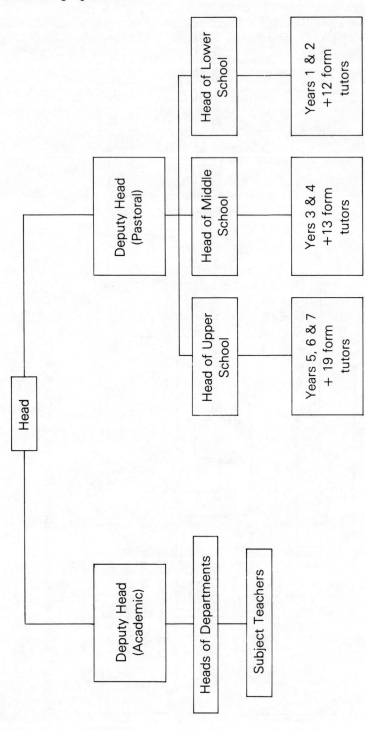

Figure 2: The school structure

should take place throughout the school. It is the responsibility of every teacher and cannot, should not, be seen as the province of only a few specialists.

The author of Figure 2 would probably argue that pastoral care is the province of specialist team leaders, but not theirs alone; they operate through the school structure shown in the diagram. We would raise two objections to this proposition.

First, the 'philosophy' underpinning the pastoral work of the school is transmitted in many unintentional ways, one being through 'innocent' diagrams. Figure 2 shows two aspects of the school's work operating entirely separately. It is clear that many of the teachers in the 'pastoral team' are also members of the 'academic team', yet no attempt has been made to emphasise the concept of this overlap or duality of responsibility.

The second objection rests in the logical inconsistency first voiced by Marland (1974) when he argued for the institutionalisation of pastoral care structures. He stated: 'It is really a truism of school planning that what you want to happen must be institutionalised'. What he failed to mention was the corollary to that argument: what is institutionalised may well happen, whether you want it to or not. We are not arguing here for the abandonment of pastoral structures as illustrated in Figure 2. We would stress, rather, that more care needs to be taken in their presentation, so as not to give the impression that certain aspects of the school's role are the preserve only of specialist staff. In Figure 2 the implicit philosophical statement made by the apparent institutionalisation of the pastoral/academic split may well influence teachers' attitudes towards pastoral care.

As well as looking at *how* ideas about pastoral care are presented, it is important to consider the content of what is being said. Figure 1, *Lines of communication in the pastoral system* reveals an apparently autocratic pastoral system in operation in the comprehensive school from which it comes. What attempt does the school make to broaden that interpretation? Their statement is lamentably brief, and is reproduced here in full.

'1 *The Second Mistress* (The Director of Pastoral Care): is responsible to the headmaster for the operation of the pastoral system throughout the school. The senior mistress, in Upper School building, acts as her deputy.

2 *The Special Unit*: caters for emotionally disturbed pupils, who for various reasons cannot be educated in the main stream.

Referral to the unit may be for a short or long period depending on the circumstances, but it is never used as a 'sin bin'.

3 *The Year Head*: there are two year heads for each year group – usually a man and a woman. The year heads are responsible to the director and her deputy for the pastoral care of pupils in the year group. Year heads have access to pupils' personal files and are authorised to issue official school detentions. They prepare reports for outside agencies after collecting confidential reports from subject teachers. Year heads are responsible for gathering the information required to make recommendations to the head-master on band transfers.

4 *Form Teacher*: should make every effort to familiarise him/herself with the pastoral needs and problems of the form members and alert the year head if he/she detects any sign of emotional disturbance or becomes aware of any significant change in home circumstances.'

Clearly, our disappointment derives from the brevity of this statement about the pastoral system. Look carefully at the specific items that have been selected for presentation in this statement. We must presume that, given the limited nature of the statement, the items chosen for inclusion take on a greater significance.

Three of the items are about roles rather than systems. We learn little from the statement about the second mistress. Of course we can assume that the school considers the role only of sufficient importance to allocate their second mistress to take charge of it; that is, the person fourth in line in their hierarchy. There are several potential inferences to be drawn from the fact that, apparently quite deliberately, the school favours women in their senior and middle management pastoral roles.

The severe limitations to the role of the head of year raise important questions about the school's definition of pastoral care. Apparently, looking at files, setting detentions, preparing reports and acting as secretary on banding reviews are the most crucial elements of the job. Whilst there is brief mention of the 'responsibility . . . for the pastoral care of pupils', there is no definition of what is meant by that.

We should not read too much into the fact that the Form Teacher is left to last. Here, too, there is a singular lack of guidance as to what 'pastoral needs' are. The two elements that are picked out – looking for emotional disturbance or changes in home circumstances – are perhaps meant to be a clue.

Perhaps the final and almost incontrovertible fact is that this brief statement about the pastoral system gives priority to the – no, not 'sin bin' – special unit. It brings us back to the oft-mentioned problem of emotional disturbance. Are we to conclude that the pastoral system in this school concentrates on picking up the problems of emotional disturbance and referring them either to the special unit or to an outside agency?

We have tried, in this opening account, to draw attention to the need for clarity in a school's statements about pastoral care. It is important *what* we say; it is important how we represent our ideas or structures diagrammatically; it is equally important what we choose to leave out – the omission of some items or the inclusion of others may give greater significance to an issue than we intend.

It is certainly true that the school would be wrong to commit ideas to paper until those ideas had been thoroughly discussed, well understood and agreed as valid through a consensus of the staff. What is written will reflect the school's philosophy in respect of the caring element of the teacher's role. For this reason it is important that we understand and have considered what that philosophical view is to be.

Philosophy and caring

One possible starting point for a school's analysis of its standpoint on pastoral care is a staff conference, perhaps for a day, or, as has been possible in some local authorities, for a weekend. The purpose would be to achieve an understanding of the pastoral system – its philosophical roots, its structure, its integration into the work of the whole school, its scope – despite inevitable disagreement on some issues.

Let us illustrate this line of thought with some examples. If the school's philosophy states that the key member of the pastoral team is the form teacher, it is up to the pastoral team to give this concept substance and meaning. What does such a statement say for them about the relationships between:

- the form tutor and the tutees;
- the form tutor and parents;
- the form tutor and outside agencies;
- the form tutor and academic monitoring?

The list seems endless.

It is important for the team leader to agree with the members of the team how this is to be interpreted in terms of their working relationship. (Notice here the echoes of our approach on issues involving the whole staff, where we argued for discussion and consensus.) Again, their stance on a particular issue may well determine their reaction under a given set of circumstances.

For example, a member of staff goes to see the team leader to complain that a pupil is not producing homework regularly; how does the team leader respond? Much will depend upon the developed relationship between the team leader and the pastoral team. In some circumstances the team leader might ask the subject teacher to approach the child's form tutor direct about the matter. In a different working relationship the team leader might make notes and promise to get back to the subject teacher when the form tutor has been consulted. What would be inconsistent with the philosophy and could not happen would be the team leader's dealing with the matter without reference to the form tutor at any time. This would be incompatible with the philosophy of the school and of the pastoral team.

It is likely, then, that one of the first tasks undertaken by the pastoral team will be to look at the stated pastoral aims of the school. It might prove a valuable exercise for the team to see how well the stated aims are reflected in practice. In the light of such an analysis, the team might propose specific ways in which they want to work in order to bring philosophy and practice closer together.

The next task is to consider how the school's stated pastoral aims are interpreted for them. As has been suggested, different styles of structural organisation, for example, might indicate a particular stress or emphasis for a particular team. 'To prepare all the children for the world of work' has a different emphasis for the fifth-year pastoral team than for the first-year team.

At this point it might be sensible for the team to try to thrash out their own 'philosophical statement'. A document entitled *Pastoral care and the fifth year*, for example, would serve a number of purposes.

- It would help to bring the team closer together in their understanding of the task and the way it is to be performed.
- It would be a useful basis for discussion with the senior management team of the school. It is important that others, not directly involved, have a chance to contribute and are allowed the opportunity to see how you will work as a team.
- It would provide for a potentially helpful cross-fertilisation of ideas, if made available for scrutiny by other teachers and teams.
- It sets a bench mark for other staff. A team of teachers trying to forge a cohesive approach, whilst it may not affect others' prac-

tice, may well affect the way that those teachers deal with 'the team'.

Such discussion in itself serves a valuable purpose in that it allows people to consider views and express ideas even though these may be founded on mis-information, misunderstanding or prejudice. The result should be a greater understanding and better informed view of pastoral issues. Even though there may be those who, at the end of the day, will disagree with the consensus viewpoint, the majority of staff will *understand* the school's philosophical statement on pastoral care.

Such an understanding would allow the staff to consider all the elements of the school's life and how they are related to the pastoral care philosophy of the school. Such a whole-school policy on pastoral care would be a way of institutionalising a pastoral care system that would be the core of the school's activity rather than a peripheral issue.

If it is important for the headteacher and the school to state their philosophy of pastoral care, it is equally important for such a stand to be taken by a pastoral middle-manager responsible for leading a pastoral team. We have already described how the school's stated approach on a particular issue may affect the behaviour of the staff (and students) when confronted with this issue. It is equally true that a member of a pastoral team needs to know where that team stands on basic matters.

The philosophy of the pastoral team must mirror the pastoral philosophy of the rest of the school. There may be elements of the team's work with a group of children (perhaps because the sub-division is on an age or familial basis) which bring into focus specific points of the whole school philosophy, and so the team should make it clear how that philosophy is interpreted for them.

The same arguments about working from a philosophical basis apply here for the pastoral team leader as they do for the headteacher and the school as a whole. By establishing a philosophical framework through discussion and consensus with the pastoral team, the team leader will bring a sense of purpose and cohesion to the work.

Where situations arise which need some reference to policy for a solution, the outcome is almost predetermined. Since the arguments and background of the philosophy are understood by those operating the system, there is a greater likelihood of a consistency of approach.

Such a clarity of purpose has obvious advantages for staff, but the students, too, will have a much clearer idea of the school's approach on a range of issues. Their understanding will come from observing, lesson after lesson, day after day, consistent practice in a given set of circumstances. It is our experience that students will be only too happy to exploit weaknesses and inconsistencies in a school's approach, to their benefit, if given the opportunity. A philosophically based management approach is much more likely to minimise such exploitation.

Exercises

1 Without reference to any source material, try to write down what your school states as its 'pastoral philosophy'.
2 Draw a diagram to show what structures, referral procedures, chains of communication and other forms of organisational systems operate within your school's pastoral care framework.
3 Write down all the points where you believe the statements, in literal or diagrammatic form, differ from the actual practice within the school.
4 For the part of the school where you have pastoral responsibility, try to write your own version of the school's statement about pastoral care, tuned, as you see it, to the needs of the students that you deal with.

References and further reading

Best, R., Ribbins, P. and Jarvis, C. (eds) 1980: *Perspectives on Pastoral Care*. Heinemann.
Department of Education and Science 1979: *Aspects of Secondary Education in England: A survey by HM Inspectors of Schools*. HMSO.
Department of Education and Science 1978: *Truancy and Behavioural Problems in Some Urban Schools*. (HMI Report) HMSO.
Hodgkinson, C. 1978: *Towards a Philosophy of Administration*. Blackwell.
Marland, M. 1973: *Pastoral Care*. Heinemann.
Moore, B. M. 1972: *Guidance in Comprehensive Schools*. NFER.
Preedy, M. 1981: 'Pastoral Care and Guidance'. In *Managing the Curriculum and Pastoral Care*. E323, Block 5, Open University.
Richardson, E. 1973: *The Teacher, the Pupil and the Task of Management*. Heinemann.
Vaughan, T. 1975: *Education and the Aims of Counselling*. Blackwell.

3   Managing the pastoral team

What is teamwork?

Both the structure and the content of pastoral care provision in the school will benefit from the establishment of a philosophical framework, within which common aims can be identified and achieved. It can provide that cohesion which comes only from a shared sense of purpose, arrived at through debate and discussion. Within whatever kind of structure the pastoral team is working, the effectiveness of that team will be increased if the importance is recognised of an agreed perception of the task and a shared commitment to the nature of the roles and functions necessary to achieve common aims through the successful completion of those tasks. The consensus implied in this view of pastoral care provision will not be achieved by accident. Each pastoral team will have to develop working relationships consistent with the overall pastoral philosophy of the school. These relationships will need to be negotiated within the team and, once established, will need to be managed. Building and managing the pastoral team is one of the prime responsibilities of the house or year head.

In any discussion of team building and managing, an understanding of the nature of teamwork is crucial but this is seldom considered. It is generally assumed that everyone knows what teamwork is. Thus, when 'pastoral team' is mentioned teachers are expected to have a shared perception of what that means. Most staff-room discussions of this matter will reveal just how erroneous that assumption is. For example, the prevalent notion of professional or staff development among almost any group of teachers will focus on developing the skills, knowledge and experience of individuals, but the key to successful teamwork is to be found in the way in which groups of teachers relate to and work with each other. Group development, therefore, should be considered as important as individual development, because individuals working together in a team achieve more than they could alone. The success of the pastoral team depends not only on the

Figure 3: Teamwork

WHAT IS TEAMWORK?

A group of people working together on the basis of:
    i Shared perceptions
    ii A common purpose
   iii Using agreed procedures
   iv Commitment
    v Co-operation
   vi Resolving disagreements openly by discussion

This will not happen automatically. Teamwork has to be managed if it is to be effective.

---

individual skills of its members but on the way those teachers support and work with each other (see Figure 3).

Teamwork has been described as 'playing from the same sheet of music'. Individuals with their own skills, experience and responsibilities as well as their own levels of commitment, personal concerns, pressures and influences work together for a common purpose, guided by a team leader who accepts overall responsibility for the development of the team, its aims, the standards it sets, and the results it achieves. This includes a responsibility for the ways in which individual team members are developing as well as a responsibility for the development of the team itself. The processes of individual staff development are not dealt with here, but reference is made to helpful sources for this in the bibliography. This chapter will concentrate entirely on exploring a model for effective teamwork which can be applied to the pastoral team. It is recognised that teams normally work through meetings and through the delegation of tasks to team members in order to maximise the use of time, skills and experience, especially in situations where there are pressures for change. Delegation, organisation of effective and useful meetings, optimum use of time, and response to pressures for change will all be dealt with in subsequent chapters. This chapter concentrates on the processes of teamwork.

If teamwork is seen as a group of individuals working together towards some common purpose and, in so doing, achieving more than they could alone, then the justification for the existence of a pastoral team in any school would seem to be self evident. Almost no-one enjoys working in a situation in which they are isolated, alienated, criticised, over-controlled, or feel frustrated and dissatisfied with their own performance as a teacher or tutor. Successful teamwork can take place, however, only when the team has the facilities required to gather relevant information, to make sound and informed decisions and to implement those decisions. The absence of any of these factors can mean that the team cannot work effectively or that it will not work at all. Lack of individual commitment can have a similar effect and so can a variety of personal issues which are not brought out into the open within the team context. Individuals may have such undisclosed aims as ambition, retribution, destruction, covert support, which they may intend to pursue within the working of the team, and it is the responsibility of the team leader to be able to identify such factors and bring them into the open as part of teamwork. Several extremely useful references for those involved in such a process are included in the bibliography.

Colleagues will contribute to the pastoral team only that which they feel, as individuals, they wish to contribute. This may include their knowledge and skills, but it may also include their dislikes and jealousies, their uncertainties and perceived or real lack of ability or experience. None of these factors needs present the team leader with insurmountable difficulties provided s/he is aware of their existence. Lack of skill may be overcome with training. Dislikes need to be aired within the team in a sympathetic and controlled way. Jealousies have to be countered by building self-esteem rather than by diminishing the worth of another individual within the team. An effective pastoral team leader will recognise that there are a number of psychological processes operating within any team, through which tutors come to identify with the team. These processes can be seen as a useful counterbalance to those factors which may make effective teamwork difficult.

Interaction between the individual and the team may take place on the basis of one or more 'psychological contracts' which the individual may make, consciously or unconsciously, between himself and the team. The interaction may be based on compliance, that is, on the avoidance of some form of punishment, isolation perhaps, or to gain some form of reward such as acceptance by the team. To the extent that the individual wishes to gain the reward or avoid the punishment, he or she will comply with what the team is doing. This need not result in passive conformity, especially if the ethos of the team is such that decisions are taken and actions planned on the basis of informed, open, analytical discussion. The interaction may be based on identification, that is, on the need to find support for some course of action which the individual may wish to pursue and which he or she regards as being compatible with activities of the team. The interaction may be based on rationality, that is, on the recognition that the individual has a problem to which the team might offer a solution or about which advice may be forthcoming from team member to team member. The individual does not have to like the advice for this form of contract to be effective. Even if such advice or support is contrary to the individual's normal role or set of expectations, such a contract can exist, provided the individual recognises that what the team is offering is logical and rational. Finally, the contract may be based on internalisation, that is, on the belief that what the team is doing, or how it seeks to perform its functions, is, in itself, worthy of support and participation. This, clearly, is the strongest form of contract and the one which is likely to generate the most commitment from the team member to the team itself. Nevertheless, the other forms of contract should not be dismissed or disparaged, provided that the team leader can identify them, recognise them for what they are, and be aware of the limitations which they imply, for it is upon foundations such as these that successful pastoral teams are built (see Figure 3).

Team development

Good teamwork will not just happen: it needs to be developed and managed. It also needs to be based on an understanding of the reasons which colleagues may have for participating in a pastoral team as they do. Each individual will participate to a slightly different extent and for different reasons, depending on the nature of the 'psychological contract' between themselves and the team. These factors constrain the extent to which tutors are prepared to be involved in the workings of the group, but they are not the only ones affecting involvement. The individual factors mentioned in the previous section are also relevant and so is the way in which tutors perceive the pastoral team itself. The way in which the team appears to operate is a crucial factor in determining how much time tutors are willing to give. People are usually more willing to commit themselves to expending their time and energy on a pastoral team if they understand clearly what they are doing and why they are doing it. This means that team leader has to understand and communicate to colleagues the rationale of the pastoral team's work. In other words, the existence of a philosophy of pastoral care upon which the working of the pastoral team is based is a crucial element in its effectiveness.

It will be clear from the way in which the school is organised, as well as from the way in which pastoral care is structured within the school, that the pastoral team is only one part of the total organisation. Realistically, therefore, there are limits to what a pastoral team can do, the problems with which it can cope, and the issues which it can address. It serves no useful purpose to have an exaggerated view about what is possible within the framework of the pastoral team. For example, neither the team nor its leader can necessarily be held responsible for the wrong people having been appointed tutors. No amount of teamwork can fit a square peg into a round hole. The team can, however, attempt to develop training programmes for those members who may lack certain skills or information. These need not be as elaborate as an in-service course but might simply be the provision of an opportunity for an experienced colleague to work with a less experienced one on a particular aspect of pastoral work. The team cannot necessarily address directly the problems created by a confused or inappropriate organisational structure in which, for example, a particular group is not functioning effectively or, conversely, is too powerful for the good of the whole organisation. The pastoral team can only try to ensure that it achieves as much as it can in the circumstances. Nor can the team deal with situations deriving from a lack of overall planning within the school, low morale in the school, an inappropriate system of rewards and promotions, or other similar problems. These are management problems which may not be capable of solution within the pastoral team. They may provide part of the context within which the team has to work and over which its members have little or no control. They do not make effective teamwork impossible but they may make it more difficult.

All members of the pastoral team have to recognise that their team is part of a larger organisation, the school. Effective teamwork on their part is only one of the factors, albeit an important one, upon which the school depends. Effective teamwork cannot solve all the 'people problems' in the school, but a well-developed pastoral team can go a considerable way towards improving the effective delivery of pastoral care within any school.

What, then, is a well-developed team and how is it achieved? The pastoral team is a group of individuals working together. Some of

Figure 4: Developing the team

TEAM DEVELOPMENT	
Objectives	The objectives of the team should be clearly understood by all members.
Procedure	All team members should be involved in making important decisions.
Process	All team members should be clear about what has to be done, by whom, with what resources.
Review	The team should review its work regularly as part of a learning and development process.

what they do is independent of the other members but much of what they do depends upon and overlaps with the activities of others. Interaction takes place smoothly, efficiently and effectively so that the general provision of pastoral care within the school is maintained and improved. This is achieved only by a careful consideration of the objectives, the procedure, the process and the membership of the team (see Figure 4), and of the ways in which the activities of the team are reviewed and monitored.

All teams, whether they be sports teams, departmental teams or pastoral care teams, are concerned about the image which they have of themselves and which others may have of them. They are concerned about the standards set and about the results achieved. Members are concerned with the extent to which they can improve and develop both as individuals and as members of the team and, therefore, they are concerned about how far their own needs, as well as those of the team, are taken into account when activities are planned and responsibilities allocated. All these concerns crystallise around the tasks which the team is expected to undertake. In any pastoral care team the members will, to a greater or lesser extent, be aware of what has to be done. Successful teamwork, however, is best achieved when the aims and objectives are clear and when all members subscribe to them. The distinction between aims and objectives in this context is a crucial one. Aims, in the context of managing a pastoral team, are best regarded as being derived from the overall pastoral philosophy and are broadly strategic in nature. To offer guidance in educational choice-making and career decisions might, in this context, be an aim. Doubtless, every member of most pastoral care teams would accept this as a proper and legitimate aim for their team. The difficulty might arise with the objectives. These are the tactics to be used to achieve that aim. They will involve decisions about who is to be involved in giving such guidance; when it is to be given and to whom; what actions are to follow the giving of that information and by whom. The objectives, then, are statements about what needs to be done, by whom, with whom, by when, to what standard of proficiency, and what should be done as a result. These are the tasks of the team. Each team member should understand exactly what is required of him/her, and should be informed about the scale and urgency of the task to be carried out. It should not be assumed that team members have this information. The leader of the pastoral team should accept the responsibility for providing that information, for checking that it has been assimilated and understood, and that the appropriate actions are taken. This is not an intrusion on the professional autonomy of colleagues but, rather, an essential part of the process of effective team management. Nothing inhibits successful pastoral work more than the perception, whether accurate or not, that one or more members of a team are failing in their responsibilities to colleagues or pupils. It is rare indeed for any teacher to believe that he or she is culpable in this respect. Pastoral teams will respond to a situation in which the nature of the task to be undertaken is discussed, agreed and fully understood, especially when outstanding disagreements about these matters are resolved before any action has to be taken.

All pastoral teams will operate in somewhat different ways, which should be determined by their different circumstances, the mix of individuals who make up the teams, and the nature of the school. It is important to recognise that pastoral teams cannot exist independently of each other, or of the school itself, nor should they seek to do so. The team's preferred way of working should be clearly understood by all members. The options are numerous but it might be that the team is organised on an open, fully participative basis. At the other extreme the team might be firmly and directly controlled by the team leader. The preferred method of operating for many teams is somewhere between those extremes and relies on a policy of encouraging all team members to be involved in all decision-making, where appropriate, within a clear and specific policy framework based on the school's overall pastoral philosophy and negotiated with and agreed by the team members. The extent to which it is appropriate to involve team members will depend on such factors as the nature of the immediate task – does it require quick decisions and action?; the style of response required by the task – to what extent does it demand clear direction or arouse emotion? When clear direction is required or when the issue is emotive, too much participation can be counter-productive. Who is affected by the issue or task? Where several team members are affected by the task, it is essential to involve all of them in key decisions. Who can make a useful contribution and who feels that they have a contribution to make? If several team members have knowledge, experience or even an interest in a particular task or issue, then it is best to involve them in making decisions about it. The appropriate method of operating, therefore, might be on the basis of a predetermined view about who should be involved or about who should take the decision to involve other team members. A team leader who has the trust and respect of the team will be able to carry out this function effectively and to ensure that the team can adopt procedures for taking decisions and carrying out tasks. The team can then concentrate on the process of achieving results.

If the procedures adopted by the pastoral team dictate how the individuals in that team operate as a group, then the processes used by the team will influence how that team sets about achieving its objectives, getting the results, and attaining the standards which it has set itself. Team processes are means of achieving the objectives which make up a task. The process of task achievement should start by ensuring that all the members of the team fully understand the aim and the objectives. How this might be done has been described in the preceding paragraphs. The processes on which most successful pastoral teams are built are likely to contain all of the following elements after the tasks have been derived from the objectives.

Thus, if the aim is to provide guidance on making educational choices, the objective might be to interview all pupils coming to the end of their third year in order to establish the best fit between the realistic career aspirations of pupils and the possible options available to them. This objective might then be sub-divided into a number of tasks: identifying what options are likely to be offered; identifying how many children will need to be interviewed and when their parents can accompany them; establishing who will be most able to carry out the interviewing and making the necessary arrangements for those interviews.

The pastoral team has moved from the stage of identifying objectives, through the stage of breaking those objectives down into a series of tasks and into the actual process of teamwork, in fact, into the realm of planning. Planning is simply a matter of identifying what has to be done, by whom, with what resources and to what time scale. It involves allocating tasks so that everyone within the team knows who is responsible for what. With those responsibilities should go the necessary authority to ensure that the task can be successfully completed. Resources, both human and material, must be analysed, known and allocated in order to meet the requirements of the various tasks in the most effective way. All too often tasks are allocated and resources deployed on the basis of tradition and common practice rather than on the basis of what is actually needed to complete the task in hand.

Timing, similarly, is important. Time is always short and needs managing. One team member's deadline may be another's start time. If the deadline is not met, the next task may not be completed on time. If, for example, letters do not go out to parents early enough for them to reply, for those replies to be translated into appointments for interviews and for the parents to be informed of the final arrangements, then the whole programme may be thrown into confusion. It is worth ensuring, therefore, that the team responsible for achieving this particular objective knows how each individual member's tasks fit into the overall programme. Perhaps one member whose sole function is to ensure that the various schedules are met – a timekeeper, in fact – should be identified. Carrying out the plans requires good communication, but it also requires that team members should listen to each other, be supportive and allow ideas and suggestions to be generated and used where possible.

Once the task has been completed the process should still continue. Time should always be allocated so that the pastoral team can review what has been done. Team review is a valuable learning and team development function. All the team members should be involved in discussing such questions as: 'Did we complete the task successfully?'; 'What went well in our process and can be repeated next time?'; 'What went badly and held us back?'. It is because these questions are important to the present activities as well as for the future development of the team that all team members should be present at such discussions, even if their roles are only marginal to the enterprise being considered. There are other review techniques which can be applied to many pastoral team activities and there is much more that can be said about delegating, allocating responsibilities, and the effective management of time. These will be considered further in Chapters 4 and 6.

The tasks of the pastoral team may change with time, and the processes to be applied in any given situation may vary, but it is important to remember that the tasks of the team form only one dimension of the teamwork. The membership of the team is of crucial significance, because it transcends any single set of tasks and persists over time, and also because any individual team member's commitment to the team and its tasks is determined, in large part, by the extent to which members of the pastoral team feel that they are, in fact, team members. Commitment to or membership of the team may vary according to the issue or the task. Colleagues will devote more energy to matters they think important. They will also give their time if they believe that they can influence outcomes or that they have something of value to offer. Membership of the team should not, therefore, be accepted at face value: it should, rather, be regarded as a variable which may need to be taken into account, reconsidered, developed and cultivated. Team members may need encouraging, reassuring and appreciating in order to establish and retain their membership of the team in an active sense. Commitment to any pastoral team in terms of time and effort cannot always be expected as of right, even if it is a part of a teacher's professional responsibility.

The effective team leader has to be aware of these recurring factors and, over a period of time, ensure that the various members of the pastoral team feel themselves to be a valuable part of that team. This can be done simply and informally by finding out from team members how far they feel able to relax in the team meetings; how far they have private reservations about team decisions; how far they accept and understand team objectives; how well the team operates as a group and to what extent influence is shared by all team members or is concentrated in the hands of a few. The effective team leader will collect much of this information indirectly by observation, rather than directly by interrogation. In the same way, the team leader will recognise the extent to which responsibility is shared within the team and the degree to which differences within the team are suppressed and denied or are identified and worked through satisfactorily. Team membership can be regarded as the single most significant variable in the development of a successful team. It has to be seen for what it is, a variable rather than a constant and, therefore, it has to be kept under review, if the team is to remain effective.

Managing the effective team

The development of the effective pastoral team is complex and is not easy to achieve. The team can be damaged by neglect, but with sympathetic and careful management it can devise processes for fulfilling its aims and objectives and completing its tasks successfully. It can also provide satisfaction for its members, but, in order to do this, attention has to be paid to four complementary factors which contribute to the effectiveness of any team. These are the individual, the task, the team and its leadership (see Figure 5). These elements form the framework within which the management of the pastoral team has to be carried out, and the team leader must ensure that a satisfactory balance is achieved between these elements.

Each individual brings to the team strengths and needs. The combination may vary but the categories remain the same. Colleagues might, for example, have basic needs related to survival and existence. Such people will be motivated by the need to earn money and, if they feel their rewards are just, they can be expected to function reasonably well. When, as in a teachers' pay dispute, a significant number of people feel that their rewards are not just, motivation may depend directly on changes related to basic rewards and nothing much can be achieved until changes have been effected. This is a fairly extreme

Figure 5: Managing the team

TEAM MANAGEMENT

Individual	The nature and extent of the individual member's commitment to the team has to be understood.
Task	The task has to be identified, explained and communicated to members and progress towards its achievement monitored.
Team	The integrity of the team should be maintained by encouraging co-operation and exploring the causes of disagreement.
	Team leadership has to be flexible, based on an understanding of what is to be achieved in particular situations.

position which is unlikely to apply in all schools with all colleagues, many of whom may identify other forms of needs and rewards. Another example might be the need for an acceptable self-image. Teachers can be helped to become valuable team members by being encouraged to become the people they want to be. Others may need to do something useful or meaningful. Clearly this need is related to self-image, but it shows the team leader that effective team management depends as much on understanding what colleagues want as on knowing what the team objectives are. Closely related is the need to belong to groups of different kinds. Few people genuinely want to exist in isolation and most people want the recognition which comes from being a valued member of a group. This can be a firm basis on which to build team membership and is particularly true when the team can also provide the opportunity for personal development and, in so doing, meet the need to grow and develop experienced by most people. This need is recognised in pupils and is often expressed in terms of fully stretching them or allowing them to reach their full potential. Teachers have a similar need. A good team leader will be aware of that and manage to provide opportunities for team members to grow as part of the team's activities.

Apart from obvious financial rewards, it is possible to provide rewards in several different ways. Those directly related to the task in hand might include more responsibility, a more interesting activity, freedom to plan and implement, or a change in working conditions, such as an office space in which to work. Perhaps more subtle than these, the second set of possibilities might include more opportunity to express a particular talent, the chance to develop or improve knowledge or skill, or the chance to exercise full control over some aspect of the team's activities. The rewards which come from team membership itself include approval, co-operation, friendship. Finally, and least obvious of all are the rewards connected to those needs which may never be articulated by the individual, such as the achievement of some long-term or idealistic aim, or the desire to earn popularity, admiration or respect from others within the team. These possibilities all provide the team leader with opportunities to manage the team to obtain the best effect both for the individual and the group.

The importance of the task in effective team management has been emphasised throughout this chapter. The setting of clear and attainable objectives for the pastoral team, allocating responsibilities within the team, identifying targets, and establishing ways of measuring the team's progress towards meeting those targets are all part of the duties of the manager. Planning to ensure that the group attains the success that its members would not otherwise achieve either as individuals or without the management skills of the team leader is, therefore, a crucial part of the role of the effective pastoral team manager. Central to this is not only the ability to identify, define and communicate the nature of the tasks to the team members but also the ability to explain why the team is performing the tasks which have been identified and the flexibility to re-define tasks and encourage the team to re-allocate responsibilities and resources when necessary. A plan is only a good plan as long as it is relevant and as long as it is taking the team where it wishes to be. Management, in this context, includes the ability to recognise when things are going wrong as well as knowing when they are going right.

When things are going right the essential task of the team leader is to maintain the team and ensure that it continues to work as a co-operative, supportive entity. But, at times, things *do* go wrong, and when they do the 'common sense' explanation frequently given is in terms of 'conflicting personalities', that is in terms of people who are so different and difficult that hostility is endemic and conflict is inevitable. This extreme form of social determinism appears to have little validity in real situations since, more often than not, it is possible to improve most situations. The 'conflicting personality' explanation, on the other hand, would indicate exactly the reverse. It might be more useful to view any threat to team co-operation in terms of a conflict of expectations rather than a conflict of personalities. Whenever the behaviour of one person violates the expectations of another it could reasonably be anticipated that co-operation might be withdrawn and conflict result. People will then attempt to hurt or punish colleagues rather than help or support them. In such a situation the pastoral team leader has to recognise what is happening and maintain the integrity of the team. This will, more often than not, have to be done by helping team members to explore their own behaviour with the intention of highlighting where the conflict in expectation is located, without attributing blame. Such team maintenance activities are the third dimension of effective pastoral team management.

The final dimension of effective team management is the recognition that the leadership role will alter as the nature of the team's activities changes. For example, the team may need firm and clear management when it has to complete a specific task within a limited period of time. Alternatively, when the team is exploring ideas and issues the emphasis needs to be on exploring the thinking of team members, encouraging all colleagues to contribute and drawing contributions together in order to build upon them. At some of its meetings the team might be receiving a briefing about a forthcoming activity. Here skills of exposition, checking understanding and the management of information are relevant. Persuasiveness, openness and patience combined with the perception to recognise the importance of what is not being said as well as what is being said might be required of the pastoral team leader when reviewing the processes for achieving a specific objective, in order to learn from what has just happened. Different management skills are required of the pastoral team leader in different situations.

These four elements, the individuals, the task, the team and the leadership role, have to be balanced by the effective manager of the pastoral team. This requires an understanding of the individuals in the team, an awareness of what is going on in the group and an understanding of what this might mean in the context of the group and its activities, the skills to act upon this knowledge, and the recognition that different actions might be appropriate in different circumstances. If members are strongly motivated to achieve results, if the team has shared standards and targets, if colleagues seek ways to improve their processes through co-operation and if individuals gain in confidence and ability through belonging to the pastoral team and contributing to its success, then the pastoral team leader has gone a considerable way towards ensuring that the basic elements of effective team management are all receiving attention.

It is still necessary to build on this, however. The team leader has a duty to assist colleagues in their own professional development as part of the work of the team and as an extension of the work of the team. This is related to delegation but it must also involve some consideration of the career aspirations of team members from their point of view. Do you, as team leader, know what the career aspirations of your colleagues actually are, as opposed to what you think they are? If you do, how far does the allocation of the duties within the team equip them to attain those aspirations? This is an especially difficult area for some pastoral middle-managers to cope with since the position to which team colleagues aspire may well be that of team leader. Nevertheless, team leaders have a responsibility to broaden and expand the experience of staff in order to prepare them for their next promotion. Delegation and the organisation of work within the team ought to be structured with this in mind. This is the very least that we should all be doing for our colleagues.

We should also be aware of the other in-service training opportunities which might be available and be sure to pass that information on to team members. Team leaders may be tempted to keep, for example, committee membership to themselves when, by asking a colleague to represent the team, not only could the team leader's work load be lightened a little but a valuable new experience could be provided for a colleague. The pastoral middle-manager may be well aware of how far his/her job overlaps with that of the pastoral deputy and be willing to work closely with that person in order to gain experience to fit him/her for his/her next promotion, but the team leader has to ensure that such an opportunity is also made available to the team members.

Such professional development of staff can take place only if the pastoral middle-manager sets aside time to talk to colleagues about their own development. Some team leaders may wish to initiate regular, although possibly not frequent, and relatively formal discussions with colleagues, while others may prefer to leave colleagues to take the initiative. However, before such discussions came about, they need to be given the same detailed attention that would be given to interviewing pupils or parents. Be sure, for example, that you are clear about the purpose of the interview but remember that you are advising rather than telling people what they might do. Make certain that you will not be interrupted during the interview either by people at the door or by telephone calls. Take the phone off the hook if you have to, or advise the switchboard that you are unavailable for a period of time. Check that the room is comfortable for both of you and, above all else, make sure that you are as well informed as you can be about your colleague, including his areas of interest, his aspirations, and the information which he may need from you. Use open questions during the interview to try to get your colleague to talk to you rather than the other way round and listen to what is being said. If you give advice only do so if you are sure that it is appropriate and accurate but if you are not certain of your facts be honest enough with your team member to say so, but offer to find out whatever needs to be discovered. Any action which is agreed upon during the discussion should be noted down by both of you and followed up. If you agree to do something, set a deadline, and make sure that you have done it and reported back to your colleague by the time agreed. This is not only an indication of your efficiency as team leader but is also an indication to your team members that you are interested and concerned about them as people and as colleagues. The professional development of the team is the responsibility of the team leader and can only be successfully achieved if the individual members of the team feel that the team leader is interested in them as individuals. Such concern makes the pastoral team a more effective unit and, at the same time, makes it easier to manage. Priorities may be agreed upon more readily, responsibilities may be allocated more appropriately, communication becomes more open and meetings can be more useful to the whole team.

Exercises

1 (a) Identify two situations in which your pastoral team worked well together and completed its tasks or attained its objectives. Why was this so?
(b) Identify two situations in which your pastoral team failed to work well together or to complete its tasks or attain its objectives. Why was this so?
(c) What are the main differences in the two different circumstances and what forces are working in favour of producing an effective team?
2 (a) List the main tasks of your team.
(b) List the main strengths of your team members.
(c) Identify which team members can tackle the main tasks.
3 Collect the data to answer the questions posed in the final paragraph in the team development section of this chapter (p. 36).
4 The final paragraph in this chapter summarises the four key elements in effective team management. Under each of the four headings:
(a) List your own strengths and weaknesses.
(b) Ask a colleague to identify your strengths and weaknesses.
(c) Identify strategies for building on your strengths.
(d) Plan a training programme for yourself to strengthen your weaknesses.

References and further reading

Adair, J. 1983: *Effective Leadership: A Self-Development Manual*. Gower.
Bradley, R., Chesson, R. and Silverleaf, J. 1983: *Inside Staff Development*. NFER Nelson.
Hamblin, D. 1984: *Pastoral Care – A Training Manual*. Blackwell.
Marland, M. 1983: 'Preparing for Promotion'. In *Pastoral Care in Education*. 1 (1), pp 24–36.

Olroyd, D., Smith, K. and Lee, J. 1984: *School-based Staff Development Activities: A Handbook for Secondary Schools.* Longman, for the Schools Council.

Richardson, E. 1975: *Authority and Organisation in the Secondary School.* Macmillan.

Scott, B. 1981: *The Skills of Negotiating.* Gower.

Woodcock, M. 1979: *Team Development Manual.* Gower.

4 The team, its priorities and their management

Managing priorities

The pastoral organisation ought to reflect the priorities of the pastoral team, although some of the messages which come to pastoral tutors about the school's attitudes and priorities are sometimes less than clear. Nevertheless, the priorities of the pastoral team are the product of the inter-relationship between the philosophy and the organisation of pastoral care within the school. Essentially, however, the priorities of the pastoral team will find their expression through the activities of that team as its members carry out their pastoral duties in the school. In view of this, it should be recognised that all members of an effective pastoral team should share in the responsibility for establishing those priorities, at least at the team level. As part of this process of taking responsibility for the work of the pastoral team, the team leader has to ensure that the priorities of the team are clarified and reinforced through a process of identifying those active, positive tasks which the team has to undertake. This requires that pastoral middle management, as well as senior management, adopts a realistic approach to the allocation of available resources, including staff time. Fair and effective delegation of duties, establishing and maintaining communication between team members, and ensuring that all members of the team are able to make the most effective use of the time available to them, are the crucial components of such a realistic approach to pastoral activity.

Management can be thought of as a combination of three distinct but related activities. Getting things done, or administration; doing new things, or innovation; reacting to crisis, or salvation. The management of any organisation or part of an organisation involves all three forms of activity, but the effective management of an organisation comes only through establishing the right balance between those activities. Any manager who is reacting to one crisis after another can hardly be in control of events, let alone be capable of managing an effective team of colleagues. It is not unusual, however, for those in middle and senior management positions in schools, as well as in other organisations, to argue that they have time only for crisis management and do not have time for innovation and the planning and thinking which it involves. Alternatively, the person who has allowed the routine administration to become such a burden that it occupies every available moment is equally at fault, as is the innovator who is always dealing with change and can never establish stability. They all have in common one failing above all others. They are unable to manage their time. The ability to do this is essential before a manager can seek to share the responsibility for the work of others. The leader of a pastoral team must, therefore, be capable of managing the time available for pastoral work.

In the final analysis, the only person who can manage your time effectively is you. It is possible, however, to establish some guidelines for the effective use of time which can help the pastoral team leader to ensure that he or she is making the most efficient use of the time available and can also help the team leader to encourage other team members to be equally well organised. These guidelines are based on the belief that, before time can be managed, it has to be analysed and planned. Before this can be done, however, it is necessary to establish what the priorities of the team are and, within those, what the priorities of the team leader are. It is only in the light of clearly established priorities that time can be managed. Those people in management positions who are unable to manage time effectively are likely to be those who have not sorted out their priorities or those who do not use those priorities in order to guide what they do.

In order to establish priorities, we must recognise that they come in different shapes and forms and do not all deserve the same amount of attention. Priorities fall into four categories. The urgent tasks have to be done now, if not before. There are far fewer of these than might be supposed, although it often takes courage and determination to admit this, because it can involve saying 'no', or, at least 'not now' to people. There are important tasks which do not have to be done immediately but which will require considerable attention: these can be scheduled so that they can be given the attention they deserve. Some tasks are both urgent and important, they require considerable attention and have to be done immediately. If a manager is confronted with many of these, s/he should ask, 'Why?' If a large number of such tasks

Figure 6: Keeping an activity log

AN ACTIVITY LOG

Method

   i Start a new sheet for each day, and use as many sheets as you need for the day.

  ii Record each separate activity in the order in which it occurs. Enter start time, finish time, a brief description of what happened and a note of the total time spent.

 iii If an activity is unplanned, but requires immediate action, mark your entry with a star.

 iv Keep the log up to date during the day.

  v If you find it inconvenient to carry separate log sheets around, use a notebook.

 vi At the end of each day's entries note anything which made that day different or caused special problems (e.g. teacher off sick).

Example

TIME FROM-TO	ACTIVITY	TIME SPENT
7.30 – 8.00	Breakfast	30 mins
8.15 – 8.35	Drive to school	20 mins
8.35 – 9.00	Deal with post	25 mins
9.00 – 9.20	Registration/tutor group	20 mins
9.20 – 10.00	Interview with parent	40 mins
10.00 – 10.45	Teaching	45 mins

Remember
An activity is anything you do, including meal breaks, driving, talking, waiting, etc.

---

regularly confronts the team leader, it suggests that such tasks should be predictable, or somebody has the wrong set of priorities, or the tasks are being dumped, that is, passed on without due consideration.

Finally, there are tasks which appear to be priorities, but which are neither urgent nor important. These can generally be left a while because they tend to be tasks which, ideally, should be done but which can be postponed until time becomes available for them. They should not, however, be forgotten. Left too long, such tasks might become urgent or important or both.

The extent to which any task should be described as urgent or important has to be determined by asking, 'What am I trying to achieve?' or, 'What is the team trying to achieve?' Once you have an answer, you can establish how far any demand on your time is important and/or urgent. If a task does not make a significant contribution to what you are trying to achieve, it is neither urgent nor important and, perhaps, you should consider whether you should be doing it at all. Most pastoral team leaders feel that they have more to do than they can fit into the time available.

The question, 'Where does all the time go to?' is often asked. To manage your time effectively you need to be able to answer that question. One way of doing this is to keep an activity log (see Figure 6). For at least three working days record all the things you do: note down every activity, the time you started and finished, a brief description of what happened and the total time spent. Keep the log up to date during the day, because if you try to leave it to the end of the day you will not be able to remember everything you did and the times will not be accurate. At the end of the day note anything which made that day different or caused special problems. Remember to include travelling, meal breaks, waiting, talking to people and time spent thinking. You can now compare the actual use of your time with how you ought to be spending it, in terms of what your real priorities are. In order to do this, identify all those items on your log which make little or no contribution to the achievement of your priorities; those which should be done by other people but which, for some reason, you are doing (even when the reason is that you like doing it or think that you are good at it); those activities which take up more time than they should or than you can afford to spend on them.

You are now in a position to examine more closely how you spend your time and to consider ways of using it more efficiently. Review the activities which you have listed on your activity log and think about how some of the activities can be reduced or eliminated. For example, is waiting a problem? Do you spend too much time waiting to see colleagues, waiting for information or searching for it? Do you make unnecessary journeys within the building or do you make journeys which are not as productive as they could be? How much time do you spend on social activities or chatting, and do you make the most of break times when everyone is together? Do you allocate specific time to necessary paperwork and do you keep the paperwork to an acceptable minimum? These are just a few of the questions which might be asked on the basis of an activity log, but remember that such a log is only as useful as you allow it to be. You can benefit from repeating this exercise every term.

Once you have completed an activity log there are three more things you can do in order to plan the use of time more effectively. First, you can seek to reduce the number of unplanned activities. Use your experience to try to spot problems before they happen. If an unplanned event seems urgent, consider what would happen if you did not attend to it. Is it really urgent? Make sure that every member of your pastoral team knows how to deal with emergencies which might arise and that they can cover for each other by dealing with the problem immediately, if necessary. As a rough guide, you should never be spending more than twenty per cent of your time dealing with unplanned activities, nor should any member of your team. If more than twenty per cent of time is being spent in this way, it is the responsibility of the team leader to try to minimise the extent to which unplanned events interfere with the smooth operation of the pastoral team's activities.

This brings us back to priorities again. Each member of the pastoral team should be encouraged to plan his or her use of time for at least a week ahead and write it down. This is not the same as the weekly forecasts which teachers are often required to make. Rather, it is an attempt to ensure that everyone in the team is using the available time most effectively. This plan should include a list of pre-arranged events such as routine meetings, teaching time and visits. Although you cannot predict which unplanned events will arise, it might be possible, with foresight, to leave some time for them in your planned use of time. The plan should also include a list of those things which you have to do but, before you can write this list, you need to look again at the priorities of the pastoral team as well as those which you, as team leader, have identified.

Bearing in mind what the priorities are, it is possible to prepare a list of tasks to be done. This list should include everything which you expect to have to do in the time period under consideration. Once you have your list, give each task a rating of A, B, or C. A tasks are those which are important and urgent for meeting your priorities. B tasks are important but not urgent, and C tasks are those which you would like to do if time allows. Having done this, you can plan your time. Do not try to do all the A tasks first because, although these tasks are important and urgent, there are other considerations to take into account. For example, can you start a task and then stop it easily, to return to it later? If not, you have to ensure that there is sufficient time available to complete it. This might mean moving some routine tasks in order to provide the necessary time. Are some of your A category tasks dependent on other people providing information or resources? If so, you have to allow time to obtain that information or those resources before embarking on that task. Do you need an item of equipment, say, a word processor? This may need to be arranged in advance. Once you have taken into account all these considerations, you can plan your use of time for the week. Remember that the aim is to match the time available to your priorities by doing first things first.

Once you have planned your time, put the plan into operation. No plan is perfect, however, and things will go wrong. Review your plan regularly and revise it when necessary. Check that your estimate of the time necessary for key or routine tasks was accurate and, if you are wrong, make a note of the actual time taken. Include in your plan time to think and plan ahead. Remember that, as pastoral team leader, you are responsible for the work of your team members. You have to find time for them. You should encourage them to make the most effective use of their time. You may even find, as you carry out your review of your own activities, that you are doing work which should or could be done by other members of your team. The work of any pastoral team should be shared. The team leader has to ensure that responsibilities are shared equitably between people able to take them on. This means more than simply allocating responsibilities: it means delegating.

Delegation

Delegation within the pastoral team is inevitable since no team leader can possibly do all the necessary work. There are, however, some things which the team leader should never delegate, although all team members should be involved in the relevant decision-making. Setting the objectives and priorities for the team must, ultimately, be the responsibility of the team leader, as must the organisation of team members, in so far as this responsibility is delegated to the team leader from the headteacher. It is also the team leader who has to accept responsibility for communication within the team and between the team and other parts of the school. Monitoring the work of the team, staff development within the team and making the routine decisions should also remain the sole province of the team leader after appropriate consultation with team members. Tasks should be delegated to team members who are or should be responsible for them by virtue of the posts they hold, because it is in the relevant job description, or because the persons concerned can be trained to carry out the necessary tasks.

Delegation is, in a very real sense, a part of staff development. More often than not in schools 'delegation' is giving away work which a superior does not want to do, cannot do, and cannot be bothered to train somebody else to do properly. If tasks were delegated effectively in schools more frequently, teachers who gain promotion would already be able to carry out most of the essential duties attached to their new post. Is this true of members of your pastoral team who are seeking promotion? It is part of the duty of the team leader to ensure that tasks are delegated effectively especially as delegation involves far more than merely giving another colleague a job to do. It has more to do with the assignment of responsibility and authority than with the transfer of a task from one person to another. Delegation should never take place without some form of training.

Training, in this context, does not necessarily mean that a teacher has to leave the pastoral team and be sent on a long-term secondment or on an in-service course. Normally, training needs prior to delegation can and should be met from within the resources of the team. This should be the role of the team leader or some other experienced team member/s. Explanation, coaching, demonstration, trial and error in a supervised situation are all forms of training which have been successfully applied in schools. The point is that training should come before delegation. The extent and nature of the training will be determined by the experience of the teacher receiving the training, the nature of the task being delegated (since a complex task will need more training and closer supervision than a simple one), and how much margin for error there is. If an error or misjudgement will have serious effects inside or outside the school, as when arrangements to discuss careers with pupils and parents are not organised properly, then detailed training and close initial supervision are necessary (see Figure 7).

Figure 7: Delegation

STAGES IN EFFECTIVE DELEGATION

Plan Delegation Decide which task you should delegate, and to whom

Assess the task and the person, to decide how much briefing and help the person requires to take on the task. Give sufficient authority to perform the task.

Delegate the Task   Brief and help the member of staff.

Inform colleagues.

Your role in following up aftet delegating should be made clear.

Check whether you are Succeeding   Check to see if you are succeeding with your delegating.

It has been suggested that successful delegation depends on four factors. Defining clearly and precisely the areas of responsibility to be delegated is the first. The pastoral team member should understand the purpose of the job to be delegated and for what he or she is to be responsible. Is the responsibility permanent or does it last for a specific and specified period of time? Are the limitations of the task clear in terms, say, of how much money is available, how much staff time can be used and how much secretarial and reprographic help is to be forthcoming? The second factor concerns the authority to carry out the delegated task. Does the team member have the necessary authority to do the job? Can he or she sign letters or use the school office or take decisions without referring back to the team leader? Third, the team member has to be clear about how his or her performance will be judged. Nobody can be expected to take on new responsibilities without making some mistakes, but performance criteria should be agreed and specified at the outset. The final factor, and the one which is most often neglected, is the direct responsibility of the team leader, who must ensure that every other team member is informed about the change in authority and responsibility. This communication helps the team leader because colleagues will no longer come to the leader for help and information about those tasks which have been delegated. It helps the team member to whom the tasks have been delegated because, by telling all relevant colleagues that delegation has taken place, the team leader is acknowledging in public that authority and responsibility have been given to the team member. Communication within the pastoral team and from the pastoral team to the rest of the school is vital to the effective management of the team, the school, and the work of the individual teachers who are members of both team and school.

Communication

Communication in schools, as in any other organisation, is an extremely complex topic and a thorough coverage of it would deal with everything from policy-making at senior management team level to individual job descriptions for each member of staff, taking in the school, departmental and team communication systems along the way. It might include formal and informal interviews with staff, pupils, parents and others and would have to look at types, patterns and the content of communication. Such an exhaustive discussion is beyond our scope here. Instead it is proposed to examine briefly those factors which inhibit or facilitate communication and to consider those types of communication which are especially relevant to pastoral teams and their leaders.

In the example of communication in the context of delegation the pastoral team leader was required to inform other members of the team about a change in responsibility brought about by delegation. Providing information for colleagues is one of the main reasons for communicating with other members of the team. Obtaining information from them is a second crucial reason for communicating, we also communicate regularly in order to request, advise, admonish, warn, and praise. Communication is essential if we are to help pupils learn, if we are to influence or persuade, negotiate or bargain. Most activity requires us to communicate with others, yet we are often singularly unaware of how our messages are coming across, of how effectively we are communicating. We ignore, all too often, those factors which inhibit communication.

The one factor above all others that inhibits good communication by most of us is the fact that we have been doing it all our lives. Therefore, we must have been relatively successful in order to have survived but the skills which enabled us, as infants, to attract the necessary attention, as adolescents to cope with the strains of impending adulthood, and as teachers to cope with the daily routine of teaching, are not necessarily those which make us effective members or leaders of pastoral teams. The fact that we have all been communicators for so long leads us to forget that we may not be as effective as we, or other people, might like. Good communication must avoid ambiguity and the possibility of being misunderstood or misinterpreted. It should not generate suspicion or hostility, since this often means that the content of the communication is rejected and we then have to deal with the anger which it creates. A pleasant letter is usually more effective and productive than an unpleasant one.

Within a group like a pastoral team there is often so much that has to be communicated that the tendency is to try to communicate too much at any one time or to communicate in a style which is neither appropriate nor acceptable. As a result colleagues can find themselves being told when they should have been consulted or being asked when they needed to be instructed. The sheer size of some schools can exacerbate this situation when, for example, it is impossible to find a team member with whom the leader wishes to discuss a matter. The team leader may write a short note which, because it is written in haste, is ambiguous, unclear and threatening to the reader but not intended to be so by the writer. From such stuff team problems grow.

Team problems which have their roots in poor communication are often the product of our attitude to the process of communication, which we often see as an end in itself rather than as a means to an end. Thus, the well-produced notice, the apt memo or the carefully chosen phrase is regarded as the epitome of good communication when, in fact, this is far from being the case. Effective communication should be understood as the link between thought and action or behaviour. It is the process of conveying hopes, ideas, intentions or feelings from person to person and, in the context of the pastoral team, this is usually done so that something can happen. Thus the sequence should be:

Thoughts ——— Communication ——— Action

A failure in communication can arise in this process when the action or behaviour which follows the communication is inconsistent with the message contained in that communication. A simple example of this is the situation in which a team member fails to comply with a request, or fails to act upon an instruction. These situations are easy to identify and, in most cases, prove relatively easy to manage. The situations in which the disjunction between message and action is caused by the sender of the message, the team leader, is far more difficult to identify and to handle.

Where, for example, a year tutor has made it clear to team members that certain problems should be dealt with by form tutors and then is found to be dealing with one of those problems instead of referring it to the relevant form tutor, how might this be interpreted? Despite the fact that the year tutor's intentions might have been good – helping a colleague known to have a heavy work-load, for example – the action of the year tutor is clearly inconsistent with her message. The form tutor concerned may interpret the year tutor's action as being inconsistent with the stated policy and may then be reluctant to act in accordance with that policy in the future. Such a situation may result in the pastoral team as a whole refusing to take seriously the year tutor's stated intention to delegate responsibility in the future. Such issues as these have to be confronted as part of the communication process within the pastoral team, if effective communication is to lead to desired actions and behaviour.

All team members need to be aware of those factors which, unless attended to, will inhibit effective communication. In particular, a team leader should be aware of the particular characteristics of those with whom communication is taking place. Any communication should be influenced by such knowledge as well as by its intended outcome. Both the sender and the receiver of the communication, whatever form it might take, should be clear about the objective of the communication, whether to inform, request information, produce action or prevent action. The required outcome of the communication should also be unambiguous, incapable of being misunderstood or misinterpreted. The team leader, in sending the communication, needs to be clear about how best to gain the outcome which he or she requires from those to whom the communication is being sent. At the same time the team leader has to bear in mind how frequently communications are issued on this and other matters. The more 'noise' there is in any school or in any pastoral team caused by frequent, or even too frequent, communications which seem to the recipients unimportant and trivial, the more chance there is of an item of communication, however important, getting lost. In short, effective communicating demands that the message is clear, unambiguous, short, and simple. It must be transmitted in a style that is acceptable and understandable. The actions which it may demand should be, as far as possible, easy to understand and easy to execute. The team leader, in adopting a communication style, has to show concern for those team members with whom he or she is communicating, as well as consistency in the process of communicating and the demands which are made on those with whom the communication is shared.

The single most important factor in effective communication is the skill of listening. The more we are able to listen to others, the more able we will be to communicate with them and they with us. Listening can be broadly interpreted to mean a general receptivity to information communicated to us, but face-to-face listening, which is the result of a process of hearing, which may or may not develop into listening, is the most important of all. If a team member believes that the views which she expresses to the team leader are received in a positive, receptive way, communication is likely to succeed. This does not mean that people have to agree with each other, but it does mean that team leaders have to devise their own listening style, which shows that they are concentrating on what is being said to them and which encourages the team member to talk rather than a style which creates opportunities for the team leader to express his or her own views. Listening has to be an active and not a passive process, which involves the listener in checking that he has understood what is being said and that there is a clear agreement at the end of the conversation on what will happen as a result of it. This should not be left to chance and should be clearly understood by both parties at the end of the discussion. Active listening leads to effective communication.

This is not to say that all communication between members of the pastoral team is or should be verbal or in the form of individual discussions, but verbal communication has its advantages. It provides opportunity for immediate feedback and for the modification of the message, if necessary. It also indicates if the message is as clear and unambiguous to the team members as it is to the team leader, who may know much more of the background than do the team members. Thus, it can provide the opportunity for team members to ask questions and allows feelings to be displayed and expressed more fully, especially in a non-verbal way. Oral communication is expensive on time, if not on materials, but, more often than not, it provides immediate feedback. It should, therefore, be used when the matter under consideration is complex or emotive, unpleasant or even personal. It should also be used to give praise or where the issue is particularly important. Remember, however, that it may be necessary

Figure 8: Programme of reports and parents' evenings
SUMMER TERM

6/4	13/4	20/4	27/4	4/5	11/5	18/5	25/5	1/6

7th term starts

Third Year
* _ _ * _ *
8   9 10

Fourth Year
* _ _ _ * _ _ _ _ *
4   5   6

HALF TERM

1   2

* *
7 8

Sixth Form
* _ * _ _ * _ * _ * _ * *   *
1 2   3   4   5 6   7

THIRD YEAR
8. *28.4.85*   1's Parents' Evening
9. *30.4.85*   2's Parents' Evening
10. *5.5.85*   Options forms to be returned to the teacher responsible for option selections via the form tutor.

FOURTH YEAR
4.   *5.5.85*   Reports to Head of School
5. *12.5.85*   Reports to Headmaster
6. *16.5.85*   Reports to parents via form tutors
7.   *1.6.85*
8.   *3.6.85*   Parent' Evenings
9. Internal examinations will be in the fortnight commencing 30.6.85. Departments wishing to set examinations see Deputy Head (curriculum) before 14.5.85

SIXTH FORM 'A' LEVEL
1.   *1.5.85*   Report blanks to subject teachers from H. of D.
2.   *8.5.85*   Reports to H. of D.
3. *12.5.85*   Reports to form tutors for organisation and completion of comments.
4. *15.5.85*   Reports to Head of School
5. *20.5.85*   Reports to Headmaster

/6	15/6	22/6	29/6	6/7	13/7	20/7	27/7	3/8

First Year
* | * | * |
5 | 6 | 7 |

Second Year
* | * | * | * |
1 | 2 | 3 | 4 |

*
9

Fifth Year
*

SUMMER HOLIDAY

*
8

5. *23.5.85* Reports to parents
7. *5.6.85* Sixth Form Parents' Evening
8. *30.6.85* Lower Sixth examination week.

FIFTH YEAR
    7.7.85 Meeting for returning Sixth Formers

FIRST YEAR
1. *19.5.85* Report blanks issued by H. of D. to subject teachers
2. *2.6.85* Reports to Head of Department
3. *5.6.85* Reports to form tutor for organisation and completion of form tutor's comments
4. *12.6.85* Reports to Head of School
5. *19.6.85* Reports to Headmaster
6. *27.6.85* Reports issued to parents
7. *7.7.85* First Year Parents' Evening

SECOND YEAR
1. *16.6.85* Interim reports available in Quiet Room
2. *23.6.85* Reports collated and fair copy made by form tutors
3. *7.7.85* Reports to Head of School; form tutors to file a copy
4. *14.7.85* Reports issued to parents

to record what is said in some way. This should be agreed beforehand and confirmed by sharing the record afterwards.

Many team leaders feel more confident when they are communicating in writing. Letters, memos, notices, reports and other forms of written communication all have their place in the workings of the pastoral team but, in order to be effective, they have to be read and understood. It is more difficult to detect errors and ambiguities in written communications, especially if the item is an incorrect entry in a school or staff handbook which has already been printed in multiple copies. Written communications do, however, have the virtue that they can be re-written many times, checked and re-checked. The appropriate phrase or sentence can be chosen to convey just the right idea and the written communication is, by its very nature and provided that the team leader keeps a copy, a permanent record. It can be sent to as many people in the same form as may be required and, if necessary, it can be sent to different places at different times. It can, of course, be considered at length and can, therefore, be relatively complex or require a relatively complex response, but the significant advantage of this form of communication is lost if it provokes questions because it is not clearly written. Such a communication is in danger of being ignored. In order to use written communications effectively the pastoral team leader has to understand that writing is not a substitute for talking. Communicating in writing is suitable for different situations and appropriate for different messages from oral communication. Where written and oral communications are treated as interchangeable alternatives, communications quickly break down.

It has been suggested that schools could make far more use than they do of visual forms of communication. The timetable set out on an impressively produced commercial timetabling board with a complex range of signs and symbols designating subjects, classes, and teachers tends to be as near as most of us come to such displays unless we work in a school which has produced its own video presentation. Some forms of visual presentations might be useful to the pastoral team leader as an aid to planning and using time effectively. A flow diagram indicating when all the major routine tasks have to be completed can help to co-ordinate activities across the team: for example, when reports have to be written, a flow diagram starting from the final date, that is, when the reports have to be sent to parents, and working back to show when all the related tasks such as comments by the form or year tutor, the subject teachers, the headteacher have to be filled in (see Figure 8). It can even show when the forms have to be printed and the basic details entered either by the office or by the teacher responsible. This can reveal where insufficient time has been allowed or where hold-ups may occur. These may then be dealt with in advance in order to try to prevent them. If the diagram includes a space in which to indicate when each stage has been completed, it can be even more useful to the team leader. This technique can be applied to almost all routine and many non-routine activities involving the pastoral team and taking place over a relatively long period of time. A micro-computer can be invaluable to store and retrieve information as part of this process (see Chapter 5).

Effective communication, then, has a vital part to play in establishing and achieving the priorities of the pastoral team and in ensuring that all team members make the most effective use of their time. It is, therefore, a worth-while activity for the team leader to review the team's communication system regularly. S/he might consider how much paperwork the team generates and ask if it is all necessary or relevant. Does it always elicit the responses and actions required? If not, why not? The team leader might check with members of the team that they understand the messages they are receiving, or indeed, that the messages are being received at all. Where this is not happening, urgent steps need to be taken, perhaps through a team meeting.

Managing meetings

Meetings are intended to be a form of communication, although many of them fail in this intention. To avoid failure, pastoral team leaders need to be clear on a few simple aspects of running meetings (see Figure 9). Successful meetings are productive and are not regarded by those who attend them as a waste of time. Of course, such a happy state of affairs can be left to chance or learned by experience, but both possibilities tend to leave colleagues somewhat disenchanted! Alternatively, team leaders can learn to plan, conduct and follow up a meeting by devoting attention to the details necessary to ensure that any meeting is fruitful.

Planning starts with a decision about what the point of the meeting is to be. What sort of meeting is it and what is to be achieved? Meetings can be defined in terms of their membership, such as a year heads' meeting or a pastoral team meeting. Alternatively a meeting might be defined in terms of its frequency – the weekly, monthly or termly meeting. Such designations give an indication of the timing and the membership of the meeting, but they tell us little about its

Figure 9: Managing a meeting

THE ORGANISATION OF A MEETING	
Plan	Know the objectives of the meeting and what is to be achieved.
Communicate	Inform team members what is to be discussed at the meeting and why.
Prepare	Put agenda in a sequence and allot appropriate time to each item. Give more time to really important items than to those which merely seem important.
Structure	Control discussion by keeping team members to the point and avoiding repetition.
Record	Summarise and record all decisions. Note who is responsible for taking action.
Remind	Send out the minutes, which list decisions and actions to be taken, by whom, by when.

purpose or function. In most cases, this is because meetings serve a variety of different functions. As a result, they tend to be long and confused affairs, where mis-communication is more common than illumination, because those attending do not recognise when the meeting has changed from one type to another. There is nothing wrong with holding multi-purpose meetings provided that the chair-person and others are clear about exactly what function they are being asked to carry out at any one time.

The simplest form of meeting is one at which information is given; where the pastoral team is briefed about changes in school policy, brought up-to-date on current events, or told about particular arrangements. These briefing or advising meetings depend largely on the team leader or the chairperson, who has to be fully informed and in control of the information s/he wishes to impart. In addition, s/he has to be able to deal with relevant questions while not being side-tracked by irrelevant ones. Thought needs to be given to providing information before the meeting since it is a waste of everyone's time to hold things up while people digest material which could have been given to them well in advance. Attention should also be given to presentation: some information can best be presented on an overhead projector rather than orally, for example numerical data such as intake figures.

Some meetings are called specifically to solve problems. They may use a brainstorming technique or, simply, general discussion to generate a number of alternative solutions to the problem under consideration. It is to be hoped that a number of solutions will be examined since there is never any guarantee that the first solution will be the best or that it will be acceptable to all concerned. Recommendations do, however, need to be made, although it is quite proper for a problem-solving meeting to suggest a small number of possible alternatives and give advice about their advantages and disadvantages. At the start of the meeting the team leader needs to present the problem clearly and structure the meeting in a way that allows everyone to make contributions. It is not necessarily those who shout loudest who can offer the most appropriate solutions.

A third common form of meeting is the one set up to persuade or influence. It takes place when a specific course of action has been decided upon, and the team has to be convinced that this is the most appropriate way forward. An example of this type of meeting might be where a team considers a new form of recording pupils' achievement – although the decision to use this approach has already been taken – because the team leader wants agreement on the particular form the record should take. This should not be confused with a meeting at which decisions are to be argued through. In this type of meeting the onus is again on the team leader to be fully informed and to be able to present information concisely and clearly. More is required, however, than a simple summary of information. The team leader may need to outline the present situation and indicate the problems, then show how the new proposal will meet these deficiencies, before asking team members to comment on the proposals.

At other meetings the main aim is to reach a decision on a particular matter. Often decision-making meetings are confused with other types in such a way that those who attend are not at all sure to what extent they are being informed about a decision, consulted about it before it is being made, or asked to make the decision during the meeting. Where a decision has to be reached, the team leader should state this at the outset. It should also be made clear how any decision will be made, whether by majority vote of all present or, at the other extreme, by the team leader after s/he has 'got a feel' of the meeting. Whatever the process, it should be known and understood. When the decision is finally reached, it should be announced in such a way as to leave no doubt about what has been agreed.

Knowing how the meeting is to proceed, by understanding the type of meeting it is and the intended outcome, can lead to more effective discussion and avoid much confusion about what is happening and what has happened. Team members need to know in advance whether a meeting is for briefing or problem-solving. They should have relevant papers before the meetings so that they can digest the information. Much time can be saved by ensuring that business is initiated by fairly brief written papers distributed well before the meeting is due to take place. By reading and discussing such papers, ambiguities and misunderstandings can be sorted out in advance, so that valuable time is not wasted during the meeting. Advance communication about the business of the meeting is a vital part of effective planning, not least because it enables the team leader to inform everybody about the objectives of the meeting. It also enables the team leader to know who may be attending. This is important for two reasons. First, it may be necessary for the team leader to discuss some aspect with colleagues beforehand. Second, the team leader will then have some idea of the size of the group.

Group size is important because there is a limit to how far it is possible to communicate with a large number of people. It is difficult to take decisions in groups of more than seven, although up to ten might be tolerable in some circumstances. It is fairly easy, however, to brief groups much larger than this. It is also necessary to have the furniture for the meeting set out in an appropriate way. It is, for example, no accident that in the House of Commons the opposing groups sit opposite each other and that the business is conducted on the basis of advocacy and debate with little agreement being reached. If a meeting is arranged in a similar way, perhaps with potential adversaries facing each other across a table, it is likely that conflict will ensue. It is far more difficult to have a heated argument with the person sitting at your side. Consideration has to be given to how the communication is to flow during the meeting. A circle helps to ensure a free exchange of ideas between members of the group but it also makes the task of chairing the meeting more difficult because there is no natural focus. If the team leader sits at the head of a table with colleagues equally spaced around it, chairing the meeting becomes easier and discussion will still take place. Alternatively, by chairing the meeting from a position in front of a semi-circle, discussion is more likely to flow to and from the chairperson rather than between members of the team. The semi-circle might be appropriate for a briefing meeting, while the group round the table might be more effective if decisions have to be taken.

This form of preparation has to take place well in advance of the meeting and it requires a clear view of the meeting's purpose. This is equally true of other forms of pre-meeting preparation. An agenda should be published, giving the time; place; finishing time; topics to be covered; and an indication of who is to introduce each topic and which papers relate to which topics. Even if the agenda does not show who will introduce a particular topic, the person chairing the meeting should know and should have checked that each person is prepared. The sequence of items on the agenda also requires some thought. It might be appropriate always to start the meeting by looking at the minutes from the previous meeting and 'matters arising', to give team members an opportunity to comment or to ask about decisions and actions taken as a result of the last meeting. Informational or briefing items should come first, so that discussion does not depend on information which the group has not yet been given. It is also a good idea to indicate why the item is on the agenda. Is it for information, for report, for discussion, for decision or as a reminder?

The combination of the shape of the agenda and the control of the meeting from the chair should ensure that those agenda items which are most important for the work of the pastoral team are the items which receive the detailed attention, while the items which might generate lots of discussion but which are really not all that important are dealt with speedily and effectively. The team might also wish to have a rule about the length of time which must elapse before a decision which it has taken can be re-considered. This is useful in situations where strong opinion prevails on a matter which can be tackled in a number of ways, like the role of the form tutor or the content of the pastoral programme. It is the duty of the team leader conducting the meeting to avoid the repetition of argument either by the same person or by different people saying the same things. A good agenda can help with this as well as being an invaluable aid in keeping colleagues on the point.

In a well-structured meeting all remarks are addressed through the chairperson and members do not interrupt each other but wait until called upon to speak. The chairperson can encourage participation by posing questions to the group as a whole, which is less threatening than asking unprepared individuals. Individuals can be approached if they have been warned before the meeting that this might happen. Open questions, to which there are no simple, short answers, produce more discussion than closed questions with simple answers. As the meeting progresses the team leader in the chair should summarise and record decisions taken and actions agreed. Where a particular matter appears unclear to the chairperson it should not be ignored or left in the hope that all will become clearer at a later stage. This rarely happens, and more time will be required to sort out the mess later. If you do not understand what has happened then it is a safe bet that most other people are also confused. The team leader must accept the risk of looking silly, if risk there is, and ask for clarification. The point should not be left until all are clear and all have agreed that they understand. Summarising points, highlighting important issues, clarifying misunderstandings, seeking further information and indicating what has been decided are all important factors in the successful chairing of meetings.

The secretary and the chairperson together should be responsible for recording what happens at the meeting. All that really needs to be recorded is what was decided. If absolutely necessary this can include voting figures, but voting should be a last resort. Where an action has been agreed upon, it should be recorded together with the name of the person responsible for taking the action and the deadline set for the completion of the task. So, it might be recorded that the team leader agreed to approach the printers about producing a new cover for the report forms and would provide costing figures from three sources to the pastoral team meeting. All meetings should have minutes, which are kept by the secretary and circulated to all members, including those unable to attend the meeting, as soon as possible after the meeting has taken place. Minutes are simply a record of what was decided at a meeting. They are not a detailed account of who said what to whom about which topic. Hansard may be a necessary part of Parliamentary procedure but most schools have neither the time nor the resources to reproduce their own versions of Hansard.

When the minutes are circulated they should not just go into pigeon holes to be forgotten. Team leaders should remind each colleague who has something to do exactly what has been agreed and what the deadline is by attaching a note to the individual's agenda or by highlighting with a coloured pen the tasks which that person has agreed to perform. Depending on when the next meeting is due to take place or what the deadline for any particular action is, it may be worthwhile for the team leader to make a note on his/her own copy of the agenda to follow up some of the points at a later date but before difficulties might arise from the non-completion of any specific task. Others might also need to be informed of the outcomes of the meeting. The head or the pastoral deputy may wish to have the minutes as a matter of course and other pastoral middle-managers in the school might also find them helpful. Some items might involve other colleagues, who ought to receive copies. A circulation list for both the agenda and the minutes is always useful. It saves the bother of writing a list or checking that you have included everybody. If you keep some spare copies of the minutes, you can always pass a copy to anyone not on the circulation list.

Effective meetings which make the optimum use of the time available are not difficult to organise if they are well planned and if thought is given to the whole process of meetings, from deciding what is to be achieved to circulating an accurate record of what was decided and what actions are to be taken. A team which conducts its meetings in this way is making good use of its time. It is also more likely to be clear about its overall priorities and how it must set about achieving them. Achieving the priorities of the pastoral team depends on the effective use of all the time available. Team members need to know how they actually use their time as well as how they should use it. Effective use of time means that the way time is being used more closely approximates to how time should be used. This has to be determined in the light of the team's own priorities. Ensuring that the total time available to the pastoral team is used to greatest effect might mean that tasks are delegated to other members by the team leader. This has to be a careful process, involving training and supervision as well as the transfer of the appropriate authority to accompany the new responsibilities. Such changes have to be communicated to all team members. The communication within the team should not be taken for granted. Team leaders especially should be aware of those factors which inhibit and facilitate good communication and know which forms of communication are appropriate in which circumstances. Taken together, these skills will enable the pastoral team leader to manage the team in such a way as to ensure that the members can make the maximum contribution to the pastoral work of the school. More especially, use of these skills will help the leader and his/her colleagues to create a context within which the form tutor can develop a coherent and effective role.

Exercises

1 Carry out an analysis of how you spend your time in the next full working week. Compare this with how you think you should spend your time, bearing in mind what your priorities are.

2 Identify all the unplanned events which confront you in your working week. Identify ways of
   (a) coping with the most time-consuming ones
   (b) having time to deal with those that might occur next week.

3 Identify one main task which you carry out at the moment which might be delegated to an identified member of your team. What criteria have you used? Plan a training programme which would enable you to delegate this task and, after obtaining agreement from your colleague, implement the programme.

4 Analyse all the forms of communication which come to you and leave you in one week. Consider how appropriate and effective they are for their purpose. What changes will you make?

5 Review all the meetings you have attended this term. How might the organisation of those meetings have been improved in order to make better use of the time? How might your own team meetings be improved?

6 Practise listening to a colleague for five minutes without interrupting, showing, at the end of the time, that you have understood clearly what has been said. Where possible, note the actions or responses which you and your colleague have agreed to make.

References and further reading

Goodworth, C. T. 1984: *How to be a Super-effective Manager*. Business Books.

Everard, K. B. and Morris, G. 1985: *Effective School Management*. Harper Educational.

Jay, A. 1976: *How to Run a Meeting*. Video Arts Ltd.

Strauss, B. W. and F. 1964: *New Ways to Better Meetings*. Social Science Paperbacks.

Trethowan, D. M. 1984: *Delegation*. Education for Industrial Society.

Trethowan, D. M. 1985: *Communication in Schools*. Education for Industrial Society.

5 Managing the role of the form tutor

Pastoral time

Central to the development and managing of the pastoral team is the task of establishing an effective role for the form tutor, since it is at form tutor level that pupils and parents first come into contact with the pastoral system of the school. We have shown in the earlier chapters that in order to create consensus within the team it is important for the team leader to discuss openly the issues which, from time to time, may confront the team members. We have also suggested that the pastoral team can be at its most effective only if it has a clear and agreed set of priorities against which to establish criteria for evaluating its management, its activities and its use of resources. This is never more important than at the point where the form tutor role is being considered. There is little point in handing down a job specification on 'tablets of stone'. The team members will operate effectively only if they have been directly involved in determining their proper role and function, as form tutors, within the pastoral system. The most significant point to emerge from the discussion is likely to be the question of time. Although the team can explore the extent to which its use of pastoral time is in accord with its agreed priorities, this discussion has to take place within the context of the amount of time allocated by the school for pastoral work. It is important that the team leader has considered this point carefully, perhaps even going so far as to enter into negotiations with the senior management about it.

Essentially, the problem arises because the question of the time factor for pastoral care work has never received appropriate consideration. In many schools, the 'form period' is the block of time allocated to pastoral work. Investigation reveals that the use of this time is, for many form teachers, far from satisfactory. Primarily, the form period is used for registration and is known by that title by many. In addition, of course, comes the great weight of paper that a school produces for distribution; letters and notes for parents, information from the PTA, school newletters and so on. This is not to say that these activities are not perfectly legitimate; they are. If you talk to the form tutor, though, you will find that they consider a disproportionate amount of their time is spent on these issues. Often, too, the assembly is squeezed into this time once or perhaps twice a week for each group of students. One form period might be curtailed to allow room for a staff 'briefing' meeting. All in all, the form tutor is left with precious little time to carry out pastoral duties and perceives this role to be secondary to meeting the demands of administration, assemblies and staff meetings. It is only natural that when the form teacher is involved in discussion about the nature of his/her role, the question is likely to be perceived in terms of the time available to carry out the task. The discussion itself will be considered by some as an additional task constituting a further encroachment into their already limited time.

Time is an issue that the school needs to discuss. It is unlikely that the team leader will be able to negotiate special arrangements for her tutors in isolation from the rest of the staff. It is not going to be an easy battle to fight; inherent in the arguments against allowing more time for pastoral care will be all the prejudices outlined in Chapter 4. The emphasis of the 'opposition' is likely to be upon the penalty to the academic work of the school of allowing more time for pastoral work. It is important, if these arguments are to be successfully countered, that the advocate assemble the salient issues systematically.

The best starting point is probably not to present arguments for a particular period of time or for a particular arrangement on the timetable to allow for pastoral work; the argument is much more likely to be productive if it centres on what activity should take place, legitimately, within the pastoral time allocated. Having established the nature and extent of the work to be carried out, we are in a position to argue for an appropriate time allocation according to two criteria. In terms of pastoral activity with pupils in groups, the argument has to be advanced on the basis of a clear understanding of what the time will be used for, why those activities are important to the pupils, and how much time is required in order to carry out those activities. Where the team leader is seeking to delegate responsibility to team members s/he needs to argue for an appropriate and related redistribution of time, having identified what can reasonably be delegated and how much time would be required (see Chapter 7). On this basis, the team leader can argue the allocation of time for pastoral work within the school. Only after this issue has been raised can effective management and organisation of the form tutor role be attempted.

Attendance and non-attendance

If we analyse some of the concerns expressed by form tutors and look at how they spend their time dealing with specific issues, attendance and punctuality emerge as important areas for attention. This is partly a matter of establishing sound patterns of behaviour that will equip the student for a work environment where laxity in this respect is considered a serious fault. It is vital that good communications with the parents are maintained; most parents will understand the necessity for regular and punctual arrival for school. Those who do not may find themselves at odds with their legal obligation to present their child for formal schooling. Certainly, where a parent has dutifully sent a child out to school, the school has an absolute responsibility and the parents an absolute right to know if the child does not arrive. This creates a dilemma for the teacher. Is it significant that a pupil has not arrived on any particular morning? Has the pupil got flu? Has s/he been involved in an accident on the way to school? Is s/he truanting?

Most schools ask that parents write a note when a pupil returns from an absence. We should ask whether this is sufficient? It might be better if parents telephoned the school on the first day of any absence; the school could perhaps set aside a particular period when the switchboard would be available to take such calls. If the form tutor's relationship with the parents is right, s/he might enquire, by telephone, after the pupil's health, even on the first day that they are away. Such an activity could be seen more as a reflection of proper care than of 'snooping'.   Absence might be an indicator of problems. If a pupil stays away from school, with or without the parents' permission, for periods of time, there might be all sorts of underlying reasons. It could be that the pupil is experiencing problems with the academic work of the school; s/he may be having problems with relationships within the peer group; it could be that the absence is symptomatic of difficulties at home; the pupil might have been encouraged by another to truant. For this reason, it is important that absences be followed up systematically and the underlying causes understood.

Truancy from school may not just involve absence from whole sessions. It is not uncommon for a student to arrive punctually for a morning or afternoon session and yet not arrive for their lesson. Such casual truancy is potentially of greater diagnostic importance than whole-day absences. This is where the school's headaches really start. In most cases, subject teachers will have a standing instruction to register the group that they take for each lesson in the week. Regrettably, some teachers do not appreciate the importance of this simple procedure and fail to carry it out. In theory, a check of the absentees from a lesson against the attendance register will reveal information about truancy. In practice, this proves to be too tiresome a task for some teachers, and it may be that quite a period has elapsed before it is revealed, often by accident, that a student has truanted. The team leader is often left with a spot check on attendance or a fire drill as the only way of checking that all students registered for the session are still present.

It is important, then, that the school develops a proper system of checking on attendance at lessons as well as attendance at school. If the school has access to a micro-computer, some programming expertise and clerical staff prepared to operate the machine, this is not such a daunting task as it might at first seem. If, for each session that the school is open, a record is held on computer file of students present or absent, the record could be checked against the class list for each lesson. This does require that there is a file with each form group thoughout the school on it. These files already exist where a school is using a micro-computer for other administrative tasks. Once established, such a file has only a twenty per cent annual turnover and so is easy to maintain and update.

The procedure would be:

1 On a prepared list, the form teacher, as well as marking the register, indicates which pupils are *absent* from school for any given session. These are sent to the computer operator.

2 By recalling the pre-prepared file the operator can quickly identify on the screen, by use of a single digit code, which pupils are legitimately absent. This may represent about ten per cent of the pupil population, but the task can be done quickly, using an on-line computer.

3 For each lesson, the subject teacher has a list of pupils who should be present and indicates on it those who have not arrived for the lesson. This information is fed into the computer, which makes immediate comparisons with the attendance register.

4 By the end of the session the form tutor is sent a print-out statement that John Smith did not attend periods 3 and 4, although he was marked present on the register.

5 The form tutor is now in a position to follow this up or to report that the pupil has a legitimate reason for being away.

Imagine the effect on casual truancy, if pupils knew that if they missed a lesson this could be almost immediately identified by using the computer, and that their form tutor would have the information before the start of the next session.

This activity is an important part of the form teacher's role. It serves as a diagnostic tool; it underlines the school's commitment to good communications between home and school; and it reinforces the importance of the form tutor as the person who takes immediate and personal interest in the individual child.

Performance and under-performance

The tutor's interest is not confined though to issues of a personal or social nature. The prime purpose for attendance at school is that pupils achieve the maximum possible in terms of their academic performance. The form tutor has daily contact with the students and is likely to know them best. There will be reports from individual subject teachers, but their perceptions of a student's work and abilities are necessarily limited. It is the form teacher who is in a position to monitor the individual's work most closely and to collate reports coming from different sources.

There are a number of ways in which the form teacher can help to inculcate good habits of study in students (see Chapter 7). A homework diary is a useful device for the form teacher to use. Even if it is not school policy for students to keep diaries of this sort, the individual form teacher is not prevented from using them with his/her form. A diary can be a useful means of communication between subject teachers, form tutor and home. Parents and teachers can be encouraged to write in the diary, emphasising that the individual's progress depends on a partnership between student, school and parent. Where problems arise, the form teacher is well placed to offer help and encouragement and to monitor the student's work. It is only by such close scrutiny that the school can be sure that it is achieving its aim of maximising the performance of each student. Such academic monitoring questions the view that the pastoral system deals entirely with the non-academic aspect of the school's work. It is a legitimate part of the form tutor's role.

Maintaining accurate records on each student as s/he progresses

Figure 10: Pupils' Records of Achievement
Part of Castle Vale Pupil Profile. Reproduced here by permission of the Head of Castle Vale School, Birmingham.

ATTAINMENTS IN BASIC ABILITIES

	(Basic Level) BI	BII	BIII	(High Level) H
COMMUNICATION				
Talking and Listening 1	Can hold conversations with work mates face to face or by phone.	Can follow and give simple descriptions and explanations. Can take messages.	Can communicate effectively with a range of people in a variety of situations.	Can present a logical and effective argument. Can analyse others' arguments.
Reading and Writing 2	Can understand and write simple notices, labels and short notes.	Can follow and give straightforward written instructions and explanations.	Can use instruction manuals and can write reports describing work done.	Can select and criticise written data and use it to produce own written work.
Visual Understanding 3	Can interpret simple signs and indicators.	Can after guidance, make use of basic graphs, charts, tables, drawings etc.	Can interpret and use basic graphs, charts, tables and drawings unaided.	Can construct graphs etc. and extract information to support arguments.
SOCIAL ABILITIES				
Working with Colleagues. 4	Can co-operate with others with guidance.	Can work with other members of group to achieve common aims	Understands own position within a group and appreciates his own actions within that group.	Is an active, decisive member of a group. Helps and encourages others.
Working with those in Authority. 5	Can follow verbal instructions for straightforward tasks and can perform them under supervision.	Can follow a series of verbal instructions and carry them out independently.	Can carry out a series of tasks effectively, given minimum instructions.	Inspires confidence in those in authority and communicates well with them.
Self-awareness 6	Is aware of own personality and situation.	Can determine own strengths, weaknesses and preferences with some guidance.	Has good basic understanding of own situation, personality and motivation.	Has a thorough understanding of own personality and abilities and their implications.

	(Basic Level BI)	BII	BIII	(High Level) H
PRACTICAL AND NUMERICAL ABILITIES				
Using Equipment (7)	After demonstration, can use equipment safely to perform simple tasks.	With guidance, can use equipment safely to perform multistep tasks.	Can select and use suitable equipment and materials for the job, without help.	Can set up and maintain equipment. Can identify/remedy common faults.
Dexterity and Co-ordination (8)	Can use everyday implements, can lift, carry and set down objects as directed.	Can reliably perform basic manipulative tasks.	Can perform complex tasks requiring accuracy and dexterity.	Can perform tasks requiring a high degree of manipulation control.
Measuring (9)	Can read graduated linear scales and dials.	Can measure out specified quantities of material by length, weight etc.	Can set up and use simple precision instruments.	Can set up and use complex precision instruments.
Calculating (10)	Can identify size, shape, order, etc. Can add and subtract whole numbers.	Can use $+/-/\div/\times$ to solve single-step whole number problems. Can estimate.	Can use $+/-/\div/\times$ to solve two-step problems. Can add and subtract decimals.	Can use $+/-/\div/\times$ to solve multi-step problems. Can multiply and divide decimals.
DECISION-MAKING ABILITIES				
Planning (11)	After demonstration, can identify the sequence of steps in a routine task.	Can choose from given alternatives the best way of tackling a task.	Can modify/extend given plans/routines to meet changed circumstances.	Can create new plans/routines from scratch, using all sources of help.
Information Seeking (12)	Can find information with guidance from supervisor.	Can use standard sources of information.	Can assemble information from several sources.	Shows initiative in seeking and gathering information from a wide variety of sources
Coping with Problems (13)	With guidance, can cope with simple, everyday problems.	Can cope with complex but routine problems. Seeks help if needed.	Can cope with unusual problems by adapting familiar routines independently.	Can offer sensitive and effective help to other people facing problems.
Evaluating (14)	Can assess own results with guidance. Asks for advice.	Can assess own output for routine tasks independently.	Can assess own performance and identify possible improvements.	Can identify others' difficulties and so help to improve group performance.

through the school is most important. The form tutor, the 'hub of the pastoral wheel', is the person best placed to maintain such records.

Various types of information need to be collected: address, parents' names, telephone number, emergency contacts, health details, date of birth and so on. On the academic side, reports from subject teachers should be filed, scores in exams or objective tests noted. Knowledge of particular strengths and weaknesses may prove invaluable when offering guidance about subject selection or career choice. A note needs to be kept of communications with the home or of interviews with parents. The school will want to keep a record not just of problems that the pupil has in school, but also of particular achievements. The form teacher may want to keep a diary record of conversations with a pupil, where it may prove of significance to that pupil's future. Of growing importance is the practice of encouraging pupils to keep their own profiles. Developing the skill of self-criticism is an important lesson for students. Encouraging them to review their own progress, analyse their feelings, set themselves realistic targets and evaluate their performance in the light of those goals can have a dramatic effect in terms of student motivation and performance. The development of 'records of achievement' as a matter of central government policy clearly has implications here (see Figure 10).

The keeping of pupil records should be seen as a constructive activity rather than a drudgery. If the student's progress in school is to be monitored accurately and effective guidance offered, this needs to be done from an informed position. It is not sufficient to have the facts lodged in the memory of the form teacher. S/he may not be available when the information is needed. Such records need to be available on file. The form tutor has an important role to play in organising student records.

Most controversial of all is the legitimacy of the form teacher's contributing to the personal and social education of the student in any systematic way. Clearly, much that the form tutor does with an individual or a group has this effect. If s/he is negotiating with the pupil following a dispute with another student or a member of staff, s/he contributes to the personal and social development of that pupil. If the form teacher organises an end-of-term party for the form or a trip to the local ice rink, s/he is having an effect on the student's social development. In discussion about problems that the student might be experiencing at home, say, the amount of freedom that is allowed the young person the teacher is doing more than alleviating the immediate symptoms of a problem; s/he is contributing to the broader development of a whole person.

Developing the person

There are few who would question that developing 'the whole human being' is a legitimate part of the school's work. It is of little value to turn out a brilliant academic mind if the person is socially maladjusted, incapable of communication or lacking in social skills. Some of what we would like to see learned under the heading of 'personal and social education' will come from the school's hidden curriculum, that is, that element which is taught implicitly rather than through a particular lesson. The way pupils are encouraged to move around the school, quietly and in an orderly fashion, the way they are expected to speak to staff and other students, are examples of this hidden curriculum in which there is a clear contribution to the personal and social education of the pupil. To what extent, though, can we leave such important lessons to chance? Should the school plan a programme of personal and social education so that it can be sure that every pupil has the opportunity systematically to develop these skills?

It has been assumed, and with justification, that a set or streamed group is the wrong environment in which to approach the question of developing personal and social skills. The form group, often the only student grouping not based on any considerations of perceived ability, is seen as the most suitable vehicle for such teaching. So the form teacher is the person to whom this task often falls. But where is consideration given to the skills needed for such a teaching task? Where do the form tutors experience the in-service training to equip them for this role? These questions are often ignored, and, as a result, form teachers are faced with teaching material that is foreign to them.

A didactic teaching style is inappropriate for this type of work, which by its very nature requires group interaction, invites open questioning of assumptions and may challenge deeply held convictions. How does the teacher whose particular teaching style is far from this mode cope with the change required of him or her? In some schools this vital question is ignored.

It is small wonder that substantial groups of teachers reject such a role, given the poor preparation and the lack of in-service training. With appropriate training opportunities and with adequate support, there is little doubt that a properly developed tutor group programme can have a beneficial effect upon the students. The poor reception amongst teachers for proposals for a tutorial teaching programme needs to be confronted by the team leader and should be seen in terms of the problems outlined above. Appropriate strategies for the development and teaching of a tutorial programme are considered more fully in Chapters 6 and 7.

Working with groups of students is one way of developing the 'whole person'. Individual casework is also an important element in this aspect of caring. Children have all sorts of problems in adjusting to school and coping with the situations that present themselves. The pastoral system has seemed often to react to problems rather than to anticipate and prevent them. The idea that some form of systematic pastoral programme of social and personal development might offer this proactive function led the early writers to believe that 'band-aid' pastoral practice could be obviated. This line of thinking has been allowed to dominate for some time. In reality, no social and personal education programme can ever eliminate the crisis work of pastoral care. That is not to say that the aims of the personal and social education programme are not perfectly laudable, but, rather, that these two aspects are not mutually exclusive.

A balance has to be established between personal and social education programmes and individual casework, not least because individual casework is time consuming. It may involve the teacher in discussion with the parents. Referral to one of the supportive agencies may be called for and this may require the teacher to attend a case conference. The process of collecting and analysing data carefully and writing up reports in a style appropriate to the agency is lengthy. Offering feedback to other teachers in the school is often important to the successful handling of a case.

In the experience of many teachers, individual casework is where the pastoral task becomes interesting. But it is the experience of many form teachers that as soon as it reaches this stage, the matter is taken from them by their team leader, a deputy head or even the head-teacher. The rationale for such action is that the form teacher lacks the time or the appropriate level of expertise to carry out the task. The time may be limited, but it is likely to be so because the school determines its priorities in such a way that no time is made available. A form teacher is unlikely ever to develop the skills required unless s/he is allowed to have 'hands on' experience.

Working with other caring agencies

No issue better illustrates the question of the extent of delegation – or lack of it – than that of which staff should have direct contact with other agencies. Can a school allow a form teacher to get his/her 'hands on' work with other agencies? We use the term agencies here to cover the whole gamut of groups that schools find themselves working with from time to time: the Education Welfare Department; the Schools' Psychological Service; the Social Services; probation officers; health visitors; the police, and so on.

The school needs to have analysed its own position in respect of liaison with other groups. This question of inter-agency liaison is not for schools alone, but it is perfectly proper for the school to instigate a review of its working relationships with other groups. How well do teachers understand the working practices of these agencies and their role in dealing with schoolchildren? Exploring these issues may provide a useful in-service training exercise for teachers at all levels within the school. How well do teachers understand the ways in which other agencies work together and the tensions that exist between them?

A useful device operated in a number of schools is to convene regular meetings with representatives from all the caring agencies, to discuss individual cases. These liaison meetings, perhaps held half-termly, work through a prepared agenda of students who are known to a number of agencies and with whom the school experiences some difficulty. The primary motive is to share experience and expertise with fellow professionals, with a view to helping the school develop effective coping strategies. The 'hidden agenda' includes liaison between other agencies (sometimes, lack of co-ordination here is frightening) and in-service training for staff.

It would be valuable for form teachers to attend sessions where individuals from their group are to be discussed. However, this raises a much wider question. If a school is prepared to allow contact between form teacher and outside agency in this very limited, though important, setting, is it prepared to go one stage further and allow direct contact between agencies and the form teacher, over individuals in their charge? There are two elements to this question. First, the agencies themselves often find the complexities of school hierarchies confusing. Agency workers need to be consulted if such a radical change is proposed, so that they have the opportunity to influence the decision. Second, it is often left to the pastoral middle-manager or a pastoral deputy to liaise with other agencies and co-ordinate contact. They frequently develop a lot of expertise in the area, and build up personal contact with the agency workers. It is important that their role as co-ordinator is maintained, even though responsibility may be delegated to others. It is probably a useful training method for them to oversee the work of individual teachers in the preliminary stages, so that the expertise and contacts can be shared and the work delegated with confidence. In this way, the form teachers will begin to appreciate that they have an important and valuable role to play, and that this role is properly recognised by members of the school's management team.

Underlying all this is the proposition that it is the form tutor who has the responsibility for supporting the individual pupil through his or her school career.

Support and guidance take a variety of forms: record-keeping; checks on attendance and punctuality; maintaining links with the home; monitoring and supporting academic performance; organising a programme of tutorial activity appropriate to the needs of the students; undertaking casework with individuals in the tutorial group; and liaising with other professional groups as appropriate.

The team leader is in a position to assess how much time the form tutor needs if the pastoral role is to prove acceptable. Record-keeping and checking on attendance will require non-contact time, as will casework with individuals. Contact with home, too, is a commitment outside the classroom and in many cases such links mean involvement outside the normal teaching hours of the school. The programme of tutorial activity, if it is to be properly organised and implemented, needs to have enough time allocated to it. This may mean some rearrangement of tutorial time, which will affect the rest of the school's work. It is certainly the case that an effective tutorial programme cannot be limited to occasional moments squeezed in between a plethora of competing demands.

If the tutors are to take on this expanded role, it is important that careful consideration be given to how the school can facilitate this. It is clear that without changes of attitude among the middle and senior managers within the school, the form tutor's role will continue to be minimised. Many form tutors will continue to see themselves as the markers of registers and the distribution point for mail. The changes envisaged do not come about by accident – nor can they be left to chance. In order to be successful, changes in the functions of the pastoral team or developments in the role of the form tutor have to be carefully managed and deliberately planned.

Exercises

1 Analyse the way in which form tutors use their form periods in your school. To what extent is the use of time based on a clear perception of pastoral care?

2 Analyse your current methods of identifying and dealing with unexplained absence from school. To what extent does the team contribute to this and what is its relationship with the Education Welfare Officer?

3 What formal and informal methods are used to provide information about the performance of students in academic subjects, for your team tutors? Which members of staff have a clear understanding of their pupils' overall academic development and in what ways does your team work to ensure that adequate monitoring of all pupils takes place?

4 Select from your files the records of one pupil who is not particularly familiar to you. On the basis of this record, construct a profile of that student – as a pupil and as a person. Discuss this with the relevant form tutor to establish how accurate a picture is provided by your records.

References and further reading

Best, R., Ribbins, P. and Jarvis, C. 1980: *Perspectives on Pastoral Care*. Heinemann.

Best, R., Ribbins, P., Jarvis, P. and Oddy, C. 1983: *Education and Care*. Heinemann.

Blackburn, K. 1983: *Head of House, Head of Year*. Heinemann.

Hamblin, D. H. 1978: *The Teacher and Counselling*. Blackwell.

Hamblin, D. H. (ed.) 1981: *The Problems and Practice of Pastoral Care*. Blackwell.

6 The pastoral team – managing the changes

Factors affecting change

Change in any organisation generally takes place as a response to a problem, or, at least, to the perception on the part of some person or group that there is a problem. The introduction of comprehensive education, the raising of the school-leaving age and the introduction of TVEI courses all fit this assumption. The development of pastoral care within our secondary schools may also illustrate this point, although it also shows that there may be a variety of different views as to the nature of the problem and the ideal solution. In schools, as in any other organisation, change can affect different aspects of organisational activity.

It may be that the whole or a significant part of the school is to be changed or will be affected by a change, as would be the case if the role of the form tutor were to expand in the way described in the previous chapter, or if a tutorial programme such as the one outlined in Chapter 7 were to be adopted by the school. The changes may be in procedures, such as introducing records of achievement, or in teacher and pupil behaviour, or in adopting group discussion as a mode of teaching and learning. The change may demand that the teacher develops a new approach to professional activity based on different perceptions and assumptions, such as those necessary in order to be effective in case conferences involving professional people from other services. The management of those changes which affect the pastoral team is often the responsibility of the pastoral team leader.

George Bernard Shaw once remarked: 'Reformers have the idea that change can be achieved by brute sanity.' But change cannot be introduced successfully simply by defining an end or a desired state of affairs and letting other people achieve it by following your plan. The introduction of any change will involve stress, anxiety and conflict. It will be muddled and will require carefully formulated plans to be modified and even abandoned. Change is a process of interaction even within the smallest pastoral team. It cannot be coped with by intuition alone. It must be the product of a rational approach which has, first, defined what the change is to be; second, has planned how to bring it about; and, third, has identified how to tell when it has been successful. Any change, however much it is needed and welcomed by most of those involved, will meet with resistance. Where the change affects the pastoral team it is the responsibility of the team leader to attempt to manage the change in such a way as to minimise the resistance, the conflict and the hostility.

The extent to which the change is resisted will, to some extent, depend on what the change is. A move from a house to a year system may produce resistance different from that encountered with the introduction of Active Tutorial Work, for example. On the other hand, resistance can be increased by the nature of the change situation and by the use of poor change techniques by team leaders.

Where the reasons for the change are not made clear or are presented in such a way as to be unacceptable to those people most likely to be affected by the change, resistance is likely to be encountered. It is far better to ensure that team members participate fully in exploring the need for change before any decision is taken about the nature and the extent of the proposed change. Agreeing on the need for change is the first stage in minimising conflict and resistance.

The second stage is having a specific set of objectives for the change, which are fully understood by those involved, and ensuring that these are communicated in a form in which they can be used to monitor and evaluate the change. In this way, all team members can check on the progress and direction of the change for themselves. This is important because any change generates anxiety and apprehension among those people who are affected by it as well as among those people who think they will be affected by it. Members of a pastoral team may worry about how a structural change will influence their promotion prospects, or about whether they have the necessary skills to cope with ATW. These concerns are often made worse by a lack of understanding about the present and future situations and by a feeling, on the part of the individual team member, that he or she has no ownership of the change which is taking place and cannot, therefore, exert any influence over it. Resistance can also be caused by pressure of work.

Having to cope with the introduction of a change is the last thing people will want, when overworked, especially if they already feel that their status, security or position is likely to be adversely affected. All this can be exacerbated by group pressure, where, for example, a union or some other group in the school opposes the change.

The team leader may contribute to the resistance by failing to involve other members of the pastoral team in the change process and by not demonstrating to his or her colleagues precisely why the change is needed and what it will involve. Such lack of specificity on the part of team leaders and others in similar positions is often a significant contributory factor in causing resistance to the changes they wish to introduce. Where team leaders do not take into account the existing work patterns and the ways in which pressure in any team will fluctuate, affecting different members at different times, they can increase the problems caused by pressure of work during the change, thus making the change process more difficult than it need be.

The process of change

Resistance to change can be minimised, but never eliminated, by involvement, by communication, by awareness, and by the nature of the process itself. Involving all the people who are going to be affected by the change provides them with a basis for understanding what is going on and an opportunity to influence the change, which, in turn, can generate ownership of it and commitment to it. Involvement also enables team members to have access to information about the change. Once people are informed, rumour and misunderstanding can be confronted and overcome. Sharing information allows discussion to take place. This, in turn, creates an awareness of what the problems, opportunities, and intentions are, which is helpful to the change process in any pastoral team. A team which is characterised by openness in its relationships, by a ready flow of communication not just between the team leader and members but between the team members themselves, and by a supportive environment in which problems and differences can be shared is likely to be able to cope with the difficult process of changing. Resistance will be lowered when people know why a change is being introduced and what advantages are likely to result from it.

If the leader of the pastoral team is to be able to manage change effectively, he or she has to recognise that the process of change management demands the ability to predict what the likely outcomes of the change are; to prepare for the change as team leader and to prepare others; to identify potential problem areas and the action required to deal with them; to implement the change itself; and to recognise and exploit the opportunities which the change process may produce. These abilities must be seen in the light of two basic questions. First, 'Is the change really needed?' and, second, 'Are the likely outcomes worth all the effort and upheaval which the change will produce?' If the answer to both of these questions is positive, the change must be managed.

To do this, two alternative types of process are available. One is based on a minimum of consultation and involvement and is carried through almost entirely by the team leader alone. Where there is pressure to change rapidly in the face of severe problems, with a minimum of resources available, the leader-based change may be appropriate but the process which will be considered in detail here is a participative approach to planned change. In the discussion of this approach, however, there will be much that is relevant to the leader-based approach to change, since any approach is more likely to be successful if it is well prepared and the plans are properly implemented.

Figure 11: The process of managing change

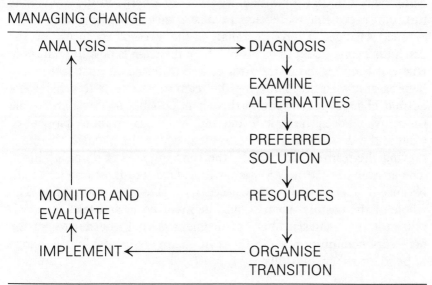

MANAGING CHANGE

ANALYSIS ⟶ DIAGNOSIS

EXAMINE ALTERNATIVES

PREFERRED SOLUTION

MONITOR AND EVALUATE — RESOURCES

IMPLEMENT ← ORGANISE TRANSITION

The participative approach to change is based on the assumption that the pastoral team is responding to a problem which it has identified or which has been identified for it. It contains several stages, each of which will be discussed in turn (see Figure 11). This should not, however, be taken to imply that every part of each stage will have been successfully and fully completed before the next one begins. Change is a complex and messy process which will not follow simple linear guidelines. It is quite likely that, during any change, several of the stages outlined below will be revisited several times. If this is the case, the team and its leader can at least be sure that they are demonstrating one of the cardinal virtues necessary for the successful management of change, that is, flexibility.

Analysis
Change will always be easier to manage if, within your pastoral team, there is general agreement on aims, division of responsibilities, fair distribution of work, effective arrangements for delegation and a reasonably efficient communication system. The importance of these factors has been discussed in previous chapters but, before embarking on any planned change, time spent by the pastoral team leader in reviewing them is time well spent. Following this, it is also worth considering the present situation in another way. If the pastoral team is in a position to be clear about the demands which are currently being placed upon it or which are likely to emerge in the immediate future, it is possible to develop a realistic view of the feasibility of the planned change. Therefore, analyse the present in terms of the demands being made; in terms of where the team is now in relation to where it wants to be in the future; and in terms of what factors are helping and what are hindering the team in its efforts to achieve the desired change. Having done this, it is possible to think about the future. What does the team leader and/or the team want to happen, or what is the desired future state towards which the planned change is moving the team? What will be the consequences of doing nothing? The answer to that question is, at this stage, the most crucial of all, because it determines just how necessary it is to change anything. The whole of the pastoral team should be involved in and take responsibility for this analysis. Such involvement is vital in order to get the necessary commitment from the team members to enable the change to be managed successfully.

Diagnosis

After the analysis comes the diagnosis of the problem. Even where a change is the result of a perceived problem, team leaders should ensure that the problem is understood fully by all members of the team. Perhaps even more important is that the team as a whole should agree that the proposed solution, the move towards which is the planned change will provide the necessary solution to the problem, as identified. It is easy for problems and solutions to become loosely attached to each other in such a way that the solution proposed, while it may be acceptable to many people on educational, philosophical or even practical grounds, may not be appropriate. For example, giving colleagues more time in which to write reports may not be the solution to the problem of late report writing if the report forms are too complex or if they require information to which year or form tutors cannot have ready access. Whatever the initial diagnosis of the problem, the team leader should seek to confirm it from a number of sources before embarking on any action. This is not a licence for inactivity but merely a suggestion that, if the initial diagnosis is wrong, everything which follows from it will be wrong. It is wise to collect as much data about the situation as possible by talking to team members and others with relevant knowledge and information, by observation, by looking at facts such as truancy rates, attendances, and all the other quantitative data that exists in schools. It can also be worth asking colleagues for their opinions about the present situation and what might be wrong with it.

On the basis of a thorough analysis of the present situation and careful diagnosis of the problem, it ought to be possible to explore solutions and the changes that will be necessary in order to move the team towards the agreed solution. Just as it was important to explore the problem in some detail and to avoid making hasty assumptions about the nature of the problem, so the same is true about identifying a solution. The team leader has to ensure that all possibilities are considered and that the first solution offered is not accepted simply because it is the first, or the most likely at a glance, or because there is support for it initially. Remember that there is no guarantee that the first choice is the best, or that the one which has the most support in the early stages will, after due consideration, be the final choice. Team leaders should ensure that as many ideas as possible are considered in the early stages. This, contrary to how it might at first appear, is time well spent.

Examining alternatives

Brainstorming is a useful way of generating a large number of ideas from within a team in a very short time. A well run brainstorm session will produce ideas ranging from the wild and silly to the brilliant and perceptive. All ideas, however, are acceptable. The brilliant ones are obviously acceptable but even those ideas which prove to be wild and silly serve several functions. They generate laughter which, in itself, is an excellent catalyst and prevents uneasy silences which are death to effective brainstorming; they also stimulate thought, which can lead the team to produce ideas which are far from wild or silly. A brainstorm is easy to arrange if a few simple rules are followed (see Figure 12). The preparation has to be carried out and shared with the team. The present situation and the nature of the problem have to be analysed as described above. The problem has to be stated to the team at the start of the brainstorm and accepted so that the session concentrates on generating solutions, not debating the nature of the problem. Team members need to have had time to think around the problem before the session, but, by involving them in the process of analysis, the team leader will already have ensured this.

When this has been done and the team is ready, the brainstorming session itself can begin. The team leader may choose to record all the ideas as they are shouted out on a number of large sheets of newsprint

Figure 12: The brainstorming technique

HOW TO BRAINSTORM

---

1   Write up a one-or two-word topic:
    Team Objectives, Achievement Records, Communication.
2   Ask for one-or two-word contributions.
3   Don't question whatever is called out, just write it up.
4   Brief the group not to challenge any idea.
5   Write up as fast as you can.
6   Give encouragement.
7   Refocus the process by picking on particular words already written up.
8   Stop when you feel you have enough material.
9   Copy list for group members.
10   Review

---

displayed in such a way that they can easily be seen by the whole group. This role does not prevent the leader from joining in. The team is asked to give as many solutions to the problem as possible. While the ideas are being shouted out, it is important that all judgement is suspended. No evaluation should be allowed of any of the ideas by, for example, making asides such as, 'That's a silly idea'. The team leader may need to enforce this strictly in the early stages, but soon the team members will themselves do so. Suggestions must free-wheel so as to allow all sorts of ideas to emerge and be recorded. What is important is the quantity of the ideas obtained, not the quality. It must be made clear to the team that they can use and abuse, develop and extend any idea which emerges. Such cross-fertilisation allows ostensibly useless ideas to be refined into good ideas as the brainstorm progresses, although no evaluation of any idea must be made until the session is over. The brainstorm finishes when no more ideas are forthcoming but the session is not yet over. The team leader asks the team to select the wildest idea from the brainstormed list. This is written up on a fresh sheet of newsprint and the team is then asked to turn it into a sensible idea by modifying it. When this process is completed the session ends. There has still been no evaluation. This comes later when the team is fresh again.

Evaluation should take place a day or two later and may be done in one or both of two ways. The whole team may assemble, consider the stated problem, and be given a typed list of all the ideas numbered in sequence. Each team member is asked to examine the list and without discussion to select about ten per cent which he or she thinks are worthy of further consideration. The leader collects the lists and identifies which ideas have the most support. These can then be considered in more detail, perhaps by a smaller group. Alternatively, a smaller group selected from the whole team can carry out a similar process, examining the original sheets and selecting the ideas which are potential winners. Each group member may then be given an idea or a group of similar ideas, together with agreed criteria against which to evaluate them. For example, the solutions may have to be implemented within a certain time, or within a specific budget, or in a certain building. After an agreed period of time the group re-assembles to consider the evaluations. This discussion should produce a list of the best ideas for more detailed analysis. If both processes are used, the best ideas from the whole team and the best ideas from the evaluation group can be examined side by side. This can be a time-consuming exercise but, where a major change is to be made, it is far better to spend time on getting it right than to repent at leisure, when it goes wrong.

Identifying the preferred solution

Out of this long and exhaustive stage, a series of solutions emerges. One of these is chosen; but this preferred choice should be subjected to further discussion. A series of questions might be asked, such as, 'In what ways can this idea go wrong?' or 'Who needs to be involved in or consulted about this?' or 'What skills and knowledge does the team need in order to implement the change, and are they available?' A more limited brainstorming technique can then be applied to generate answers which can be taken into account at a later stage. The fourth stage in the management of change process, that of identifying a preferred solution which will be acceptable to the members of the team and will effectively cope with the future situation, is now complete. On the basis of this, plans can be prepared to implement the change.

The plans for managing the change should take into account those steps which have to be taken in order to get from the present state to the desired future state. The plans should also recognise that there is an intermediate stage between the present and the future: the transition state. Team leaders and their teams should appreciate a fact that appears to have been largely ignored in the educational world, perhaps because of the way in which education uses time as a discrete barrier through which pupils pass at the end of the academic year. This is that change involves the passing of time and that, as time passes, a variety of tasks associated with the management of the change have to be accomplished. While this is going on, the day-to-day running of the school and the part played in it by the pastoral team, has to continue. Routine does not cease in order to accommodate the process of change. Therefore, after the diagnosis of the problem which leads to the identification of the solution to be implemented, the effective manager of change will devote some attention to the fifth stage in the process, the management of the transition.

Managing the transition

The secret of successful transition management is to create a structure staffed by people whose main responsibility is to ensure that the change is successful and that it takes place as smoothly as possible. They should not necessarily be those who will be responsible for running the changed situation. Transition management structures are temporary and should be disbanded when the change is complete. The team leader may wish to choose a small group from within the team. Such a group might include the 'natural' leaders in the team or those with special and relevant skills. Perhaps one person is particularly good at handling difficult colleagues, while another is renowned for organisation skills. The team leader should be associated with this group but not necessarily part of it, since the rest of the work of the team has to continue and will require much of the team leader's attention. The transition management group will have special responsibility for making those organisational arrangements which are necessary for bringing about the change, starting with a plan.

Planning may be handled by the transition management team alone, although it is likely that the team leader will be fully involved and that the rest of the team will participate in the process, for it is at this fifth stage that rumours start, anxieties develop and misunderstandings occur. Effective communication is vital and a wide understanding of what is afoot is important. By involving team members in the planning of the change these things can all be achieved, at least in part. A plan, in this context, contains detailed statements about who is to do what and by when. It should state exactly and specifically what has to be done and how those activities are related to achieving the desired change. Responsibility for carrying out the action should be clearly and unambiguously stated, remembering that a responsibility shared can provide two people with an excuse for not doing something. Tasks should have to be carried out by a specified time according to identified performance criteria which will be monitored by a member of the transition management group. The discrete activities need to be linked to show where the performance of one task depends on the completion of another. Sequencing of this kind can prevent bottlenecks and delays.

The plan should, however, be adaptable so that it can cope with unforeseen problems which will arise and those tasks which, in spite of everyone's best endeavours, will not be completed on time. The plan should be seen to be cost effective in terms of time and people. It must be remembered that everyone within a pastoral team involved in the management of change, including the transition management group, has his or her normal teaching duties to fulfil and that the change imposes additional work. This may be enriching or rewarding. It may be regarded by the team leader or his or her superiors as a vital and necessary part of staff development.

Implementation

Once the plans are formulated the change process can move, at last, to the sixth stage, which is the one at which many inexperienced managers of change in our schools want to start – the implementation stage. By identifying tasks and fixing responsibilities, by specifying deadlines and performance criteria, the team and its transition management group now has an action plan which can be implemented. But no change can be implemented successfully unless it has the commitment of a number of significant individuals, and unless it is more or less acceptable to all those likely to be affected by it. The team leader has to be sure that this is the case before the implementation process starts. Commitment and acceptance are integral parts of the same set of attitudes. Acceptance implies a willingness to let something happen without opposing it, while commitment implies a willingness to play a positive role in bringing about the change. Significant individuals have to be committed to the change, while a majority of those affected have to accept it. The most effective way of gaining acceptance and commitment is to ensure that there is general agreement about the nature and importance of the problem together with an understanding of how the proposed change will alleviate the situation. Beyond that, it may be necessary for the team leader or the transition management group to cope with a number of barriers to change. These are often expressed in verbal forms, such as, 'I can't see that working here', or 'We have tried all that before'. There are effective retorts, but such statements are often an indication of hurt or anxiety. These hurts and anxieties have to be talked through and dealt with as part of the process of managing the change. They should not be ignored, nor should they be allowed to assume undue importance. By involving colleagues from the outset, such problems can be seen early and can be minimised. Sharing information tends to minimise anxiety and reduce the effect of rumour. Nevertheless, by using meetings, individual discussions, seminars and brainstorming sessions, difficulties can be confronted and overcome. All these techniques can be used to influence, to persuade and to negotiate with colleagues involved in the change process.

Successful implementation depends on effective planning and on ensuring that the benefits of the change are recognised by those doing the work (see Figure 13). Where team members are spending their time and energy on a project, they should see, if not benefit from, the results of their efforts. This may mean that they have to be told what is going on, how well the plans are working, as well as where the

Figure 13: Implementing change

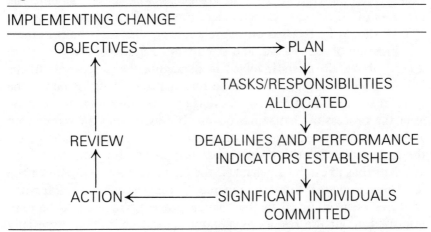

IMPLEMENTING CHANGE

problems are. The team leader has to ensure that team members have the training and support necessary to implement the change. The implementation stage of managing a change requires as much time and effort as the other stages but, by this time, team members are often running out of energy or being distracted by other tasks which need attention. The team leader must ensure that the implementation is followed through according to the plan, where necessary reminding those who have accepted responsibilities. It is helpful if one member of the group, possibly the one who is monitoring progress, also ensures that communication is effective at this stage. Are those people who have to give approval for actions being consulted? Are those people who should be informed of actions being involved? Are the appropriate and promised resources forthcoming? Are the changes which are taking place still moving the team in the direction in which it wishes to go? This, above all else, must be constantly monitored, especially in the later stages when some of the changes already made may create situations which were not foreseen in the original plan.

Monitoring and evaluating
Monitoring the change is the final stage in the process of change management but, as has been shown above, it is an essential and integral part of the whole process of change. Monitoring has to be done on the basis of the original agreed definition of the problem, the identification of the preferred solution, the plan of action designed to bring about this desired future state and the implementation of that

plan. Furthermore, monitoring and evaluation can be used to boost energy and motivation for the change as well as to examine the progress of all or part of the change process. Evaluation during the change should be focused on the relationship between the priorities, the direction of the change, and the intended desired state. The team leader, above all others involved in managing the process of change within the pastoral team, has to be sure that the change is taking the team in the desired direction and that the priorities remain the same after the process of change has begun. It may be that the monitoring and evaluation raises some questions about the change, in which case, the team leader, working with those responsible for transition management, has to establish what else they need to know, why they need to know it and what they are prepared to accept as evidence. Everyone who has been involved in the change process will need to be kept informed about the results of monitoring and evaluation, especially those leading to some modification of the original plans for action. By keeping people informed and involved, the pastoral team leader can minimise anxiety and, therefore, reduce the possibility that resistance will develop during the process of change.

The evaluation of the results of the change, that is, after the process is thought to be completed, may need to take place over an extended period of time. This, of course, will depend on the nature of the change and the intention behind it. If, for example, the change was the phasing out of a year system and the introduction of a house system, perhaps so that members of pastoral teams could get to know pupils across the age range better and, therefore, work more effectively with the older pupils as they move through the school, then evaluation will take several years. If the change is the introduction of a new system of writing reports, evaluation may take less time. Summative evaluation of this type may well take the team leader and others responsible for the change back to the original problem, the evidence which was produced to form the basis for the decision to change, and the facts and opinions that formed part of that evidence. The evaluation will have to examine, on the basis of comparing the new state with the old, how far the change was successful in achieving what was intended. The criteria for evaluating the change need to be derived explicitly from the objectives for the change established at the start of the process, which may have been modified as the change was implemented. The management of the change process is not complete until this has been done.

Leaders of pastoral teams will, almost inevitably, be faced with situations in which they are required to bring about changes in their teams or in which their pastoral teams will be involved in changes within the school. Managing change is difficult because change itself generates tension, conflict and anxiety within teams. By adopting a planned approach to change, based on the assumption that change should be an activity which is shared by all those who are likely to be affected by it and which should be managed by a few for the benefit of the whole team, pastoral team leaders can formulate an approach which will enable their teams, their colleagues and themselves to cope with the process of managing change effectively and efficiently. If team leaders are prepared, with their teams, to devote time and effort to the management of change, then it can be done successfully.

Exercises

1 Select one successful and one unsuccessful change with which you have been involved. Compare their significant similarities and differences. Try to establish why the successful scheme succeeded and why the other failed.
2 Identify one possible change which you expect your pastoral team to have to make in the next two years. What is the worst thing that could go wrong in this situation? What would be your desired future state?
3 Using the change which you identified in exercise 2, list those factors which may prevent the change being successful and those working in the team's favour. How can you minimise the effect of the former and maximise the benefits of the latter? Can you reach a situation in which the forces for, or advantages coming from, the change outweigh the factors inhibiting it?
4 For the same change, or another of your choice, draw up an action plan for implementing it, stating what has to be done – when, by whom, and to what standard. Have you the necessary resources to carry through this plan?
5 For the same change draw up a list of criteria which you would want to take into account in order to monitor the success of the change:
    (a) while it was taking place;
    (b) after the process had been completed.

References and further reading

Beckhard, R. and Harris, R. T. 1977: *Organisational Transitions: Managing Complex Change.* Addison-Wesley.

Hewton, E. 1982: *Rethinking Educational Change*. Society for Research into Higher Education.
Rawlinson, J. G. 1981: *Creative Thinking and Brainstorming*. Gower.
Taylor, L. T. 1980: *Not for Bread Alone; An Appreciation of Job Enrichment*. Business Books.
Winkler, J. 1981: *Bargaining for Results: A Handbook of Tactics and Techniques*. Pan.

7 Managing the development of the tutorial programme

The importance of influencing others

One of the most difficult tasks facing the pastoral middle-manager is that of developing and introducing a tutorial programme. This task requires all those skills discussed in Chapter 6 in the context of managing change, not least because, given the nature of pastoral work in schools, it is more than possible that the pastoral curriculum will be misunderstood by staff at all levels. A tutorial programme may be perceived as a self-contained activity of no relevance to the rest of the curriculum. Form tutors may be suspicious of the changes in teaching style that might be required of them in presenting tutorial activity. They may, too, be concerned about coping with materials with which they are essentially unfamiliar. Many tutors will already have substantial responsibility in other areas of the school's activity and may be concerned about the additional call of tutorial activity on their overloaded time. The pastoral team leader has to work on a number of fronts.

One of the starting points is at senior management level. The argument has to be established that a tutorial programme will be relatively unsuccessful if it is confined to one year group or cohort of students, or if it is developed in isolation from similar programmes working elsewhere in the school. To be effective, it must relate closely to other classroom activity, which itself is a reflection of the school's overt curriculum, and to the ethos of the school as an expression of the 'hidden' curriculum.

Whether or not this argument is accepted, it is important to try to influence the thinking and practice of other pastoral team leaders. Given what we have said about the need to coordinate such activity across the school, in an ideal setting there should be close links between pastoral teams as a tutorial programme develops, appropriate to the needs of the whole school.

It is equally important to establish links with subject departments. If we are trying to establish a learning experience for the students which is relevant and cohesive, the tutorial programme should not develop in isolation from the students' other experiences. This type of cross-curricular, whole-school planning may not readily be accepted by teachers with subject responsibilities. The pastoral team leader will need all the skills of negotiation that s/he can muster.

Working with the form tutors

One of the important routes into this inter-departmental problem is through the form teachers. It is this group, which by its very nature is most likely to be cross-curricular, that may offer the best hope of affecting curricular links with the subject departments. This group, then, is the one which must be sold on the idea of developing a pro-gramme of tutorial activity. It is this group which, for the reasons out-lined above, might be most sceptical. But it is this group's support that the pastoral team leader must be most conscientious about harnessing.

We have discussed ways of managing the pastoral team. One of the most important lessons to learn is that it would be a gross error to present the team of tutors with a *fait accompli*. There may be some benefits in looking at commercially available packages of tutorial material, but there are alternatives which merit consideration. Cer-tainly, to walk into a tutor's meeting and present the team with such a package, proposing its use as the tutorial programme, would not enhance the possibilities of its being effectively operated.

The first step with the form tutors is to engage in discussion about the nature of what a tutorial programme is trying to accomplish. 'What skills do we want our pupils to have when they leave us?' is the kind of general question likely to generate a lively discussion. The technique of brainstorming might be appropriate in this context. What should develop is the understanding that what students learn from school is not confined to the factual content of their academic studies. We are, partially at least, trying to offer skills and attitudes that will enable young people to cope with adult life. Understanding themselves and others is a starting point. They need to appreciate, for example, how decisions are made; how to relate to other people in an effective and caring way; how to manage themselves, financially and socially; the nature of social responsibility and how to exercise such responsibility in a variety of settings: as students, as members of a family, as spouses and parents. Your brainstorm session is likely to generate a much more exhaustive list than the few ideas we have offered here.

Having generated your list of ideas (and note that these are ideas which 'belong' to your team and are therefore likely to be valued by them) you have to explore the extent to which learning experiences of this sort are available to your students. The question may not be, simply, 'Are such learning experiences available to our students?', for it may be that students are exposed to such material at a differential rate. Is the academically able pupil, studying a traditional course perhaps leading to external examinations, experiencing the same learning opportunities as a pupil of lower ability who spends part of the time engaged in more practical activity? What the team is exploring here is, in fact, the pastoral curriculum. As we have defined it before, this is partly the element of the taught curriculum which offers some of the experiences itemised above.

It would be short-sighted in this discussion to consider the pastoral curriculum as that which takes place only in the classroom. You will need to explore with your team the extent to which some of these learning objectives are fulfilled through the experiences and opportunities offered by the school outside timetabled time. Consider the experience from the pupils' perspective. From the moment they walk through the school gates in the morning, how are they treated? Are they offered access to buildings and facilities before school starts? Are they expected to conform to a strict régime of school uniform? Are they offered opportunities to exercise leadership and responsibility for their own affairs, perhaps through a school council, a student-run tuckshop or a common-room committee? Is there any opportunity for them to take responsibility within the school through a monitor system, leading sporting teams, running clubs and activities, participating in a debating society or taking an active part in form meetings or assemblies?

The discussion needs to be informed. Your team may not have all the answers to the questions that they pose. It may be necessary for them to research in order to establish the answers to these questions. They may need to discuss with their departments the learning experiences that are offered to the students and the extent to which these experiences are available to all. They may need to observe the school experience from the student perspective: it might help to talk to the pupils about their experience of school.

Developing a tutorial programme for a year group

We have already stated that, in developing a tutorial programme, you will need to work within a whole-school framework. If other teams are developing tutorial activity or, indeed, if they have chosen to do nothing planned in tutorial time, that should affect the way that you devise your programme. However, for the sake of this argument, we shall consider the development of a tutorial programme for just one year group, accepting that it is a simplistic approach. It does nonetheless illustrate some of the ways in which the task might be approached. For this exercise we have chosen the first year in a secondary school, not because it is particularly easy, but rather because it illustrates the extent of the possible links between the tutorial programme, the taught curriculum and the other non-timetabled activity in the school.

A brainstorm session might be the appropriate way of discovering the themes that your team would want to pursue with the first-year group. These are some of the ideas that they might come up with:

> Understanding the geography of the school.
> An introduction to members of staff that the first year would come into contact with.
> Conduct in and around the school.
> Being prepared for lessons and learning to organise study.
> Homework.
> Understanding oneself.
> Learning to work and cooperate with people.
> Making the most of the school and its facilities.
> Learning to take responsibility.
> Making parents feel welcome in school.

This is not an exhaustive list but it will serve as a useful starting point. The next stage is to consider how each of these areas could be explored:

Understanding the geography of the school
- Pre-transfer visits to enable the pupils to get some idea of the nature of the institution they are to join. Making sure they know where to report on the first day of term. Where possible, introducing them to their form teacher and form group base.
- A guided tour of their classrooms on the first day.
- Ensuring that subject teachers escort the class to their next lesson

for the first week or until they are familiar with the geography of the building.

- Making copies of the students' individual timetables, one for them and one for the form teacher.
- Making sure that pupils know where to go for help when they get lost.

An introduction to staff
- When will students meet the form tutor, year tutor, subject teachers, the head and deputies?
- How can they be helped to understand the role of different teachers?
- When will they meet the staff from the school office?
- Do pupils know where to go in case of accident or emergency?

Conduct in and around the school
- The need for rules.
- The school rules and their purpose.
- Politeness and courtesy to others.
- The concept of a community, both inside and outside school.
- Care of the environment.

Being prepared for lessons and learning to organise study
- Knowing the timetable.
- Having the right books and equipment for the day.
- Taking essential equipment to lessons.
- Being mentally prepared to learn.
- Setting learning targets.
- Keeping a diary of progress.
- Self-assessment of progress.
- How do we learn?

Homework
- The importance of homework.
- Organising a homework programme.
- Getting help from others at home.
- Sharing learning experience with the form group.
- How do we revise?
- How to strike the right balance between work and leisure.
- Learning that is not directly related to school work.
- Leisure-time activities.

Understanding oneself
- 'Who am I?' – the student in the family context.
- 'Where do I come from?' – the student in the geographical and community context.
- 'What are my skills?'
- 'What are my weaknesses?'
- 'Where am I going?' – the student's hopes, ambitions, aspirations.
- 'How will I know when I have arrived?'
- 'Do I have opinions? Where do they come from?'
- Self and group image.

Learning to work and cooperate with people
- Understanding other people.
- Learning to listen.
- Working in small groups.
- Working as part of a team.
- Resolving tensions and disputes.
- Helping others.
- Learning to care.

Making the most of the school and its facilities
- What has the school to offer?
- School clubs and societies.
- Starting special interest groups.
- Valuing everybody's skills and expertise.
- Extending personal interests and trying things out.

Learning to take responsibility
- What does it mean to be responsible?
- Taking responsibility for oneself.
- Taking responsibility within the form group.
- Wider responsibility within the year group.
- Taking responsibility in teams and clubs.
- Our responsibility within the school community.
- Our responsibility within the local community.

Making parents feel welcome in school
- Seeing parents/teachers/students as a cooperative team.
- Bringing parents' experience into the classroom and talking about careers, parenthood, community work, the problems of being adult.

- Enlisting parents' help in clubs and activities.
- Discussing how parents can help with learning.
- Getting parents' help with form projects.
- Considering parents as students.

This list is neither definitive nor prescriptive. Given that each school is 'unique' and its staff bring to bear their own ideas, experience and emphases, the range of solutions is potentially limitless and no one solution is more or less meritorious than any other. These ideas will have been generated through a collaborative effort of the staff. Their ownership of the ideas will be an important factor in the successful implementation of the tutorial programme. Additionally, it will have been an exercise in which all could participate, even the most dogged cynic.

Looking for links

We have already said that the ideal is to establish links between the different elements of the pupil's learning experience in order to present a relevant and coherent programme. Probably the most important teachers in this respect are the subject and form teachers for the year group. This is not likely to be an unmanageable team since many of the form teachers will also teach this year group.

Many of the themes presented above could and should be followed by all the teachers who come into contact with the year group. Nonetheless, these themes need to be spelled out and agreed by the teaching team. It is far more likely that you will gain consistency if all teachers are involved in discussion about these themes, if the subject teachers know that they are joining a concerted effort and have the active support of the form teachers, and if lines of communication are established so that monitoring and evaluation can take place. Take some of the examples given above. *The school rules* should be applied consistently as students move around the school and from classroom to classroom. Students will be quick to exploit inconsistencies in the enforcement of rules and will learn negative behavioural patterns instead of positive ones.

Being prepared for lessons is a process that will start first thing in the morning with the form tutor, but must be followed up by all subject teachers as the student goes through the day. 'Have you got pens and equipment with you for the day?' 'Have you got the correct books with you for today's lessons?' When a pupil arrives for a lesson unprepared, the form teacher must know as soon as possible; s/he is then in a position to follow up the incident: by ensuring that the pupil does not repeat the behaviour, and also by using the incident as a discussion point and object lesson with the whole form group at the next form period. The students learn also that unacceptable behavioural patterns are noted and actioned by all staff, and this prevents them from playing one member of staff off against another.

Encouraging students to improve on their previous performance is second nature to most subject teachers. However, as part of a concerted effort by all staff, it can be a useful technique in encouraging students to fulfil their potential. If, as part of the teaching routine, students are helped to identify short-term learning targets, and these are followed up by form teachers, there can be a considerable effect upon student performance. This could be at a comparatively simplistic level such as encouraging one pupil to improve his or her handwriting, a theme that could be followed through all lessons. Another pupil might have difficulty in reading; if all staff are aware of the reading problem and set appropriate reading tasks as part of that individual's learning programme, improvement is almost inevitable.

Such a proposal implies devoting resources to diagnosis and communication. Clearly, the form teacher has a key part to play here, receiving input from all areas and being, therefore, uniquely placed to exercise a co-ordinating role. It is the pastoral team leader's responsibility to ensure that all students are kept under constant review. Regular case-conference meetings with individual form teachers and, where possible, subject teachers are essential if this work is to be carried out effectively. (We seem a long way now from the classic interpretation of the pastoral team leader's role as disciplinarian.)

Not all the themes are as general in nature. Some have implications for subject content. For instance, 'Who am I?' is a theme that could form the basis for a unit of work in a number of subjects. It might well form the basis for some written work in English, for individual or group projects in art or in biology. 'Where do I come from?' is a useful theme for local work in history and geography. Some of the issues under *Learning to work and cooperate with people* may have implications for teaching style in a number of subjects. Team and small-group work might well indicate appropriate classroom organisational styles.

Starting special interest groups or school clubs and societies may well be rooted in departments. An electronics or horticultural club may be an offshoot of science. The history department might well run a local history club to which pupils of all abilities could contribute.

Choirs, orchestras and bands allow ample opportunity to involve considerable numbers of students. The PE department might not only organise teams in a variety of sports, but also encourage participation in a range of other recreational activities: squash, golf, swimming and ice-skating.

Departmental staff might keep in mind the aim to involve parents in the life and work of the school. This might be in the parents offering direct input into lessons, assemblies or form periods, but could also take the form of parents acting as helpers in the classroom. Parents might volunteer to staff the library, to listen to students read or act as ancillary helpers in an art or domestic science classroom. All departments need, in a co-ordinated fashion, to actively encourage parental support and involvement. The ways in which direct parental involvement in helping the child's learning programme has had a marked beneficial effect on pupil performance are well documented.

There are, finally, several themes which could form the basis of activity to be carried out within the form period. We have already identified a number of areas where form tutors and subject departments need to work closely together, and time should be set aside for these tasks. Much of the rest of the form tutorial time could be devoted to following specific themes or groups of themes, through the school year.

Under the heading of *Learning to work and cooperate with people* form teachers could set aside regular periods, perhaps weekly or fortnightly, to allow individuals or groups of students to take responsibility for the group. This might take the form of an individual talking about one of his/her hobbies or special interests. It could be a pupil who is a keen philatelist, or a gifted musician, showing others in their group what they can do. This might allow a pupil from a different ethnic or cultural background to talk about their religion, their country of origin or the differences in customs or family life. Students who have joined clubs or societies in school might be given the opportunity to explain to others what is involved and what they have learned from the experience.

Allowing students the opportunity to demonstrate leadership or to take responsibility is an important part of the learning process. This should start in the form group, in ways described above, but might be more overt. Appointing monitors, in rotation, to collect the class register, clean the blackboard or take care of noticeboards in the classroom is an important element of this task. Under the theme of working in groups, students might take responsibility for part of the school grounds. Keeping an area clear of litter, or having a part of the school flowerbeds that the form group takes responsibility for could well provide substantial motivation.

The encouragement of good study habits and academic monitoring are important issues for form teachers. We have already said that they receive input from a number of quarters about pupil progress and difficulty. They have also the task, say, through a student daily journal, of encouraging the students to organise themselves properly. This journal might include details of homework to be done. The students might be encouraged to set themselves targets for the week and assess, retrospectively, the extent to which they met those targets. Such targets might be personal: 'I will not be late for school this week', or 'I will try to cooperate with Simon Smith rather than argue with him', or might be directed towards study: 'I will improve my work presentation in Maths this week', or 'I will learn a page of

Figure 14: A weekly programme

WEEK 15	Monitors for the week	
	Register	Sally Jones
	Noticeboard	Billy Wyatt
	Blackboard	Satwinder Panesar
	Homework books	Errol Bannis
MONDAY	Journal Session: Check entries	
	Check parents' comments	
	Activity: Students to make this week's entry.	
	Check in detail: William Lander, Molly Wilson, Steven Beeson, Rajwant Kaur Bains.	
TUESDAY	Final preparation for year assembly to be taken by class.	
WEDNESDAY	Assembly	
THURSDAY	Review of assembly	
	Mr Wyatt (Father of Billy) to talk to form group on 'My work as a fireman.'	
FRIDAY	Talk: Sally Jones and Jasmine Sotoluwe on 'Joining the electronics club'.	

French vocabulary by Friday'. Such a journal not only provides a focus for the form teacher and the student in the tutorial time but might also provide a valuable contact with parents. The journal might be taken home at weekends, to be returned, with signature and comments from parents, on Monday morning.

As each of these ideas is explored by the pastoral team, we soon begin to develop a programme of work and activity that will adequately fill the tutorial time throughout the year. A typical week's programme for one form teacher might read as in Figure 14.

Some of the themes included in your tutorial programme might need support materials and resources. Packages of commercially-produced tutorial activities are available, but if our suggestions are followed it would not be appropriate to use them extensively. Some of this material could, however, be adapted for your own purposes. Alternatively, one or two members of the team could write material for use in form periods. Writing work for use by others provides excellent experience for staff. The material can be tailored to the specific needs of your school and your programme; it can be updated and amended in the light of experience; and, most importantly, it has your team's stamp of ownership on it and is likely to be received much more enthusiastically by the tutors than would an anonymously produced package of work brought in by a publisher's rep. Clearly, however, there will be constraints on the amount of time available, which may well necessitate drawing on a mixture of different sources.

Arguing for resources

You are now in a strong position to argue your case with your school's senior management team. Look at the effect you have had on the quality of the experience for your year group and their teachers. You have persuaded departments to review their programme of work; there is now much more consistency in the work being done by the children and there are clear links in the work between subjects and the tutorial period. The year group is following a deliberate course during tutorial time aimed at enhancing both academic performance and personal and social development. You have encouraged individuals and groups of children to take responsibility in and around the school and have encouraged extra-curricular activity. Your children are developing self-motivation, are critical of their own performance and are approaching school with enthusiasm. You have involved a whole range of parents in the life and work of the school. There are a number of resources that you now need and are in a strong position to argue for.

Time

Is the block of time allocated for the form period adequate? If you are allocated, say, a twenty-minute session each morning, during which time the form tutor is expected to attend to all the clerical and administrative elements of their work, you may care to argue for some redistribution of time. You can argue that your form tutors are having a substantial impact on the performance and the personal and social development of the students. On this basis, it could be suggested that some teaching time be re-allocated to extend the form period to thirty minutes a day. Alternatively, you might like to propose that the administrative and tutorial elements of the form teacher's role be made explicit and separate. This could be done by reducing the so-called 'form period' to a registration and administrative period at the start of each session, with a tutorial programme of thirty minutes at the end of each school day. Such a 'revolutionary' proposal may not be accepted willingly, and you will need to justify it by demonstrating how you have successfully developed your inter-disciplinary tutorial programme, and the potential benefits to the students.

The second time issue arises from the need to provide adequate space for your form teachers to carry out their considerable role. This again is unlikely to meet with instantaneous support. You have to see the problem from the point of view of the headteacher. If time is to be allocated to this valuable activity, where is it to come from? You might argue that a redistribution of free time, taking periods from, perhaps, some of the more senior staff, would be an appropriate solution. Whoever is to lose the time is going to 'fight their corner' at all costs, irrespective of the merits of your proposal. We have said repeatedly in this text that, if form teachers are to perceive their role as being more than that of dealing with the tedious clerical aspects of the work, some such reorganisation is essential. Do not forget that your form teachers, if you have prepared the ground thoroughly, will support such a scheme. The suggestion that the question be put to the whole staff as an important issue of policy, might provide an opportunity for your form tutors to express their strength of feeling.

Capitation

In some schools it might be considered strange that pastoral staff actually need an allocation from capitation. You and your team of tutors, though, are now in a position to demonstrate that you need materials for pupils to use during the tutorial programme: file paper, journals, homework diaries and so on. You also need to purchase at least sample copies of texts relating to this sort of work. Again, you need to prepare your case carefully.

In-service training

Your school will almost certainly have some policy about in-service training for staff. You need to ensure that pastoral care features in that policy. There is now a range of courses, both short and award-bearing, that your staff need to go on. Such training could add significantly to the expertise of your team.

Do not, however, neglect to mention the amount of in-service work you have been doing with a whole range of teachers, in developing the tutorial programme and systematising the pastoral curriculum. Throughout the exercise your team and the subject teachers involved with them have developed their ideas about pastoral care and the issues relating to the personal and social development of their students. You need now to extend this argument to suggest that some in-house in-service programme would be an appropriate way of sharing this experience and further developing the expertise of the staff. During the summer term, when many students have left school, a volume of 'free' time is generated for the teachers of fifth- and sixth-form classes, which could be valuable as in-service training time for your tutors.

In conclusion, we probably need to restate the importance of this element of the year tutor's role. In many schools, the pastoral team leader is seen as the ultimate disciplinarian. With such limited terms of reference, the pastoral care in the school, which so clearly could have a major influence on the performance and development of the students, is unlikely to rise above the mediocre. Given the prejudice and low status attributed to pastoral care, even by some of the most senior of staff, you should anticipate that it will take time and effort to alter these perceptions of your role.

Exercises

1 This chapter outlines one way in which a pastoral programme might be developed. Examine your own pastoral programme and, with your pastoral team, explore ways of identifying those areas which you wish to change to meet the needs of your own situation.

2 After you have agreed on the areas which need to change, produce a programme which meets your needs more closely than the one you use at present.

References and further reading

Baldwin, J. and Wells, H. 1979: *Active Tutorial Work* (1–6). Blackwell.

Blackburn, K. 1983: *Head of House, Head of Year.* Heinemann.

Bulman, L. 'The Relationship between the Pastoral Curriculum and the Academic Programme'. In *Pastoral Care in Education* Vol 2, No. 2, pp 107–113.

Button, L. 1981: *Group Tutoring for the Form Teacher.* Hodder and Stoughton.

Lang, P. and Marland, M. 1985: *New Directions in Pastoral Care.* Blackwell.

NAPCE 1986: *In-service Training for the Pastoral Aspect of the Teacher's Role.* Blackwell.

Pring, R. 1984: *Personal and Social Education in the Curriculum.* Hodder and Stoughton.

8 Conclusion

The way forward

Whilst offering a brief summary of the contents of the book, we have modelled the final chapter in such a way as to make it a 'plan of campaign' for the pastoral team leader intent on changing the working environment.

To briefly reiterate what this book has attempted to do: we aim for a readership among the pastoral middle-managers or those aspiring to that post. Thus, it is largely applicable to teachers who are currently heads of house or heads of year in comprehensive schools or those who intend to move their career in that direction. It is of direct relevance also to heads and deputies, who, if they do not already know it, have a responsibility for making the pastoral care within the school as effective as possible. Although we anticipate that such senior staff will declare that they already understand and encourage effective pastoral care, we have tried to indicate that many of them have little experience and even less training in this field, and such complacency needs to be broken down.

We have not attempted a detailed critique of the pastoral care structures employed in schools. There are those who would advocate that a vertical system, a year group structure, a subdivision into horizontal 'schools' or arrangements for family groupings, offer the best organisational environment for pastoral care. For those who wish to enter into such a discussion, texts already exist which cover this ground admirably. Our assumption is that our readers will be working within an existing structure and will find it difficult to encourage change in the way that they or their team work, let alone in the whole organisational style of the school. We have suggested instead that they work within the existing structural framework of their school and attempt to make that organisational system work more effectively.

We have assumed, too, that the environment in which they work offers low status to pastoral care; this is the experience of many of the teachers we have talked to. Their own perception of their role may not be highly developed and it is likely that they are seen, by colleagues, as serving as little more than a disciplinary resource for others, who have more important tasks than mere care and control.

We have argued strongly that a successful school is one where pastoral care is seen as central to the work of the school, in that it facilitates a proper learning environment for the students. We have suggested that the role of the pastoral team leader has to do as much with the curricular style and structure within the school as with control. The curriculum of a school cannot be defined as what goes on within subject teaching classrooms, but should imply a cohesion of the experiences offered to the students. Those experiences include subject teachers' input but, more importantly, embrace the personal, social and moral education of the students. The school curriculum starts as the students leave home in the morning; it includes, quite legitimately, their experience of the school and what it has to offer, before school, at break times, lunch times and after school. The curriculum contains much about relationships and the way in which members of the school community relate and react to each other: student to student, students to teachers, clerical and cleaning staff, visitors to the school and so on.

Of major significance are the points we make about how the formal curriculum is planned and orientated. We have suggested that a division into a rigid system of departmental areas may be administratively convenient but mitigates against a cohesive learning experience for the students. We have proposed that schools need to re-evaluate the way they develop the learning content of lessons and try to plan a taught curriculum that offers a relevant and holistic programme. The starting point of any such planning must give due regard to the perception of the students. Similarly, the teaching styles and approach must offer sufficient variety and range of experience to keep students motivated. If the pupils spend most of their day sitting at desks engaged in mindless copying tasks, the school should anticipate a growing disaffection among its clientele.

As we have already stated, subject content and curriculum are not synonymous. Students learn as much from the environment in and around the school as they do in classrooms. The school needs to review carefully what it offers the students outside lessons. The environment of the school, the range of facilities and activities, the approach of the school on issues such as uniform, rules and arrangements for students at break and lunch times, constitute the 'hidden curriculum' which is potentially just as valuable a learning source as anything that takes place within a classroom.

Specifically, we have tried to identify for the pastoral team leaders management skills that they will need to develop in order to work with their team effectively. We have proposed situations where these skills might be practised and, through examples and exercises, suggested ways of acquiring them. Clearly, their success in this respect will be affected by the environment in which they work. It is unlikely that they will be able to adjust the way they work without, partially at least, changing that environment. Thus, we have proposed strategies for evaluating their situation, identifying the need for change, and instituting and appraising a change programme.

Assessing the situation

Where are you?
This evaluation falls into three phases: Try to decide where you stand on the 'landscape' of pastoral care development. Are your views founded on the perception of pastoral care as being concerned only with control? Do you see yourself as the 'expert' in discipline and order? Do you spend much of your day dealing with other people's discipline problems, patrolling corridors, toilets and cloakrooms? With the addition of a gold star and two six-shooters, would you be just as much at home in a Spaghetti Western?

Are your views based on your experience of the needs of pupils with problems? Is much of your time taken up with extensive counselling sessions of individual children who are finding school hard to cope with for one reason or another? Has your in-service training been limited to courses on counselling in schools? Is your guidance to members of your team limited to suggestions for 'getting to know your group as individuals'? This second phase of pastoral care development is no less important than maintaining a disciplined environment in the school, but, similarly, does not represent the full development of the pastoral role.

Perhaps your ideas about pastoral care place you more properly within the third stage of development, where, accepting a need for control and counselling, you also have a role to play in terms of the personal and social development of your students. This will certainly mean that you have considered the way that your students' 'pastoral period' is occupied. You may have been on a course on personal and social development and you may have tried to introduce personal and social education into a tutorial programme. How much influence have you had, though, on the broader curriculum of the school? Have you succeeded in initiating a review of the personal and social education content of the whole curriculum? Have you established a 'whole school policy' on the pastoral curriculum?

Finally, and most importantly, in the context of this book, to what extent do you see your role as a manager? Do you accept that you have a responsibility to guide and lead others, instead of undertaking the task by yourself in isolation from your team? Do you utilise a range of management techniques in order to encourage and enhance the work of others? We offer a more detailed analysis of the way your team works in the section *Changing the situation* (see p. 116).

Where is your team?
If your team is going to work effectively, it will rely heavily upon your understanding of their perceptions of pastoral care and pastoral responsibility. It will be of little value talking to a member of your team about the importance of developing a whole-school approach to the pastoral curriculum, if their practice demonstrates a primitive understanding of the pastoral care role.

Your first task is to establish the views and attitudes about pastoral care of each member of your team. At this stage, you do not attempt to change those perceptions. You need to have a clear picture of where each of your team stands on the developmental landscape. Only then will you be able to work out a strategy designed to bring them nearer to the sophisticated perception of pastoral care that you will need.

Such an appraisal can be made from your observations of your team members at work. It is likely, though, to reflect your perceptions as much as their practice. It may also be that their ideas and their practice are not coincident: they may need your help to develop their skills so that they can put into practice the style of working that fits their ideas. The best way to discover their stance in relation to pastoral care is to spend a session or two in conversation with them. You will need to decide in advance what it is you want to know and write yourself an agenda for these sessions. You will be using the interview techniques described earlier.

Where are the key figures in your school?
We have said that you will need to assess the overall school environment in terms of the sophistication of the ideas on pastoral care currently evident. What is the attitude of the head and deputies to

pastoral care? Are their statements about the importance of pastoral care genuinely meant or just rhetoric? Are there other pastoral team leaders who, like you, are prepared to take a new look at their role? Are there perhaps, amongst that group, some whose practice you would want to emulate? It is only when you have carried out this assessment of the 'pastoral climate' that you will be in a position to assess the size of the problem facing you. This assessment process must precede any decisions about action.

Much of what you do may depend on the style of management in the school. If there is, for example, a tradition and routine of regular consultation within and between teams, you will find it much easier to institute change than if your team first has to get accustomed to working in a team setting. You must make some assessment of the way that your school is currently managed in order to assess the impact of the proposed change to your own style.

Analysing your own current practice
Have you thought in depth about how you manage your own team? We are often critical of the way our own 'masters' manage us as members of their team. In the cold light of day, do you do any better? Of course, you are probably not the best person to make such an assessment. You almost certainly think that you know what you are doing and you probably have a fair idea of how others see you. Is this how you come across, though? You've probably been critical of your own head at times when he seems to say one thing and then proceeds to do another. Are you guilty of the same fault?

The people in the best position to provide such information are the members of your team. This critical exercise can be very threatening, both for you and for your team members. It is threatening for you, because you are deliberately laying yourself open to criticism. You must, therefore, be prepared for the shock when you realise that you do not apparently perform in the way that you thought you did. It is threatening for your team since, first, they will not believe that you are serious; our profession is unused to processes of self-evaluation. You will need to convince your team members that you mean what you say and that you genuinely want their help in improving your performance. Second, they will be anxious that you are not really open to criticism and that, if they say what they feel, their comments will not be welcomed and you will hold a grudge against them for speaking their mind.

We would suggest that you employ a three-stage approach to this problem. Having convinced your team to help you – and you must be prepared for some of them to refuse – offer them a questionnaire to complete about the way you work. For the sake of your own sanity ask them to include some positive as well as negative feedback. Your questionnaire might include some of the following questions:

How well do I operate as a team leader?
- Am I always consistent in the things I say?
- Do my words and deeds always match up?
- Do I offer clear leadership to the team?
- What are the things that you would like me to do better?

How well do I run meetings?
- Are my meeting agendas clear?
- Is the purpose of the discussion always clear?
- Do I encourage all present to contribute to discussion?
- Do you feel I manipulate meetings for my own ends?
- Do I always follow up decisions taken in meetings?
- How could I improve the quality of the meetings I run?

How well do I deal with my team on a personal level?
- Do I project a caring and concerned approach to staff?
- Am I sensitive to the needs of the staff?
- Do I offer support and help in appropriate places?
- Do I listen properly?

How well do you understand what I am trying to achieve as team leader?
- Do you understand my broad aims in developing a team approach?
- Do you understand my attitude to pastoral care?
- Do I present a coherent picture consistent with my aims?
- Do my aims match what you understand to be the whole-school policy?

You may think of other areas of questioning that you would want to include, or perhaps exclude some of the suggestions above. Be careful to limit your team a little in their responses. Offer them, say, a maximum of six items, three positive and three negative, so that they will distill their thoughts carefully to offer only those elements which they feel to be significant.

When you offer your team members their questionnaire, explain to them the second phase of the exercise. While they are completing their questionnaire, you will try to predict what their answers will be. This will test your powers of perception. You may harbour anxieties about the way individuals perceive you which are, in fact, groundless. You might, too, be overly confident about the reactions of some towards you.

You will need to allow an hour for the third phase. This will be an informal interview session between you and your individual team member. The object of the exercise is to compare notes to see how closely your two perceptions match. This offers a learning exercise for you both: you will understand better at the end of the session how you perceive each other. You will know, too, what your strengths and weaknesses are seen to be and you will be able to discuss with your team member what you can do to improve the working relationship. You have to be prepared, of course, to defend yourself when you are criticised for the way in which you work when you are in a position to justify your practice. You may have contradictory answers from different team members and you will need to justify what you do. One of the authors during such an exercise was told by one team member, 'you are never sufficiently accessible to either staff or kids', whilst another complained, 'You are too accessible. Your office door is always open and this tends to devalue your position and status.'

At the end of such an exercise you will have achieved a number of things. You will certainly know better how you work as a team leader. Your staff will appreciate what you are trying to do because of the time you have spent with them discussing the matter. There will be an improvement in your working relationship with your staff, and the team will work better as a result. Finally, you will have a much better idea of what motivates your individual team members.

The sophistication of pastoral practice

The final stage of this analysis is to try to assess how sophisticated pastoral practice is in your school. How well defined is the role of the form tutor? Are your tutors given a proper definition of their role. Are they given time in which to carry out their tasks? Are they given genuine responsibility for their students or are they limited to clerical tasks, with other more senior staff taking over when problems emerge?

How is the curriculum planned? Do the pastoral teams have an opportunity to provide the 'pastoral perspective' in curricular discussions? Has any attempt been made to identify the areas of the curriculum which contain the 'pastoral' content and to assess its availability to all students?

What of teaching styles and approaches? Are students offered a variety of learning environments which include full use of resources, visits, and an appropriate mix of individual and co-operative work? Is the curriculum planned in such a way as to provide cross-curricular links, affording a more coherent and relevant learning experience for the students, or is the timetable still rigidly blocked into subject teaching units with little cross-referencing?

What are the commonly held attitudes towards pastoral work in the school? Is pastoral care seen to be a responsibility of all teachers? Are pupils who experience problems in the classroom seen to be the concern of the subject teacher and the department or are they merely labelled 'problem children' and referred to the pastoral team for remedial action?

Have you tried to develop a tutorial programme for your students? Is this programme tailored to the needs and interests of your students or have you bought in a commercial package of tutorial material? How have your tutors responded to the challenges of a different content and style of approach in this unusual teaching situation?

Changing the situation

Identifying the need for change
When you have completed this assessment of the ways in which your team and school operate the pastoral system you may have a long list of things you want to change. The first task is to group these under headings such as 'curriculum issues', 'attitudes to pastoral care', 'the team', and so on. Your own list will dictate the headings that you use for this classification process. Try to limit yourself to five or six headings at the most, otherwise you will find yourself daunted by the task.

From these categories you will need to draw up a list of priorities. There will be some elements of change that you can influence directly and it may be worth considering making these your top priorities. It is only when you have demonstrated the ability to change practice in areas where you have some control that you will be able to argue effectively for change in other areas.

How are you going to get there?
Your starting point should be the working of your team. We have said repeatedly that your team members need to be convinced of the need for change and to be encouraged to involve themselves in this process.

Without their support and co-operation you will find it almost impossible to affect the way that the school operates. You will need to call upon and develop all the skills and management techniques outlined in this book. The task of managing your team, establishing priorities and goals with them, team building and development are all vital to your success.

The most threatening part of the exercise for you is to open up the discussion with your team and to allow them to contribute. If you are perceived to be approaching the problem with preconceived notions and your own 'private agenda' you will soon lose the confidence and respect of your colleagues. You must ensure that what you are doing is consistent with what you say you are doing. You will recall that 'ownership' of ideas is an important principle. If your team is allowed the freedom to contribute freely and creatively and if any initiatives on which you agree are based largely upon their input and ideas, you are much more likely to achieve your aims than if you attempt to impose your views.

The soundest piece of advice is to take the process of change slowly. Don't be too ambitious in what you and your team attempt to do. It is far better to effect small changes that are successful and breed enthusiasm for further work than to take on such a massive task that you report back to each team meeting of the failures of your agreed programme. Success breeds success and will help to encourage and inspire your team to do more. Further, if there is resistance to the change, which you can anticipate from some as a matter of course, it will be better to be seen to be making small changes in practice than to be making change for change's sake.

How will you know when you get there?
The process of change follows a cyclic pattern. There are four elements: monitor, evaluate, review and amend. You have gone through this process already by monitoring your own practice and the pastoral work within the school. You have evaluated the data you collected and, through a process of review, you have identified priorities for change. Having initiated this change in an attempt to amend the practice, you now need to complete the cycle.

As a routine part of your work with the team, you should set up ways of monitoring what you are doing. You could accomplish this by making some of your team responsible for collecting and evaluating data as the programme of reform is initiated. These team members can report back to your regular team meetings on how the work is going.

You may, in the light of a review, feel the need to amend and thus restart the cycle. The cycle should be built into your style of work as a matter of routine.

As you go through this continual cycle of renewal you will be aware when you have accomplished your aims. It may be that you begin a second initiative only when you are sure that you have had reasonable success with the first project. In this way you are able to develop a rolling programme of change that progressively alters the way in which you and others work within the school.

Professional development – conclusion and beginning

We do not suggest that your motivation for wanting to assess the way in which you work is promotion. Nonetheless, this may be the effect. All the skills of management that you have learned from this book are as applicable at higher levels within the teaching profession as to all other managerial situations. By learning such techniques and applying them successfully you will have prepared yourself for promotion.

There will still be areas of experience that you lack, if you are looking for promotion. It is worth talking to the head and deputies about their jobs. You will soon identify skills and experience that you need to acquire if you aspire to a similar post. Volunteer to work with those people, in such a way that you can observe how they function and even take on some of the tasks yourself. You should find the senior staff only too willing to help in this respect. After all, they do have a responsibility for the professional development of their staff. Not only will you be learning new skills, you will also be marking yourself out as someone who has an extended view of teaching as a profession, and is therefore a candidate for promotion. When you come to complete that application form, you will have the support of your senior staff and the confidence of knowing that you have prepared properly for the post.

The teaching profession is bad in providing such training. It is often the case that a newcomer to a job has little experience or expertise in the work. All they can claim is that they were good at their last job and so should be able to manage the next one. This leads, unfortunately, to a situation where staff are promoted through successive levels of the profession until they reach a job which they cannot do. This tendency results in schools having a range of senior staff who may have been very successful in previous jobs, but who are incompetent at the task they are now expected to undertake. By actively learning, as outlined above, you will probably not be grouped with this unfortunate minority of your colleagues.

Do not lose sight of your own team members. They will undoubtedly have developed considerable professional skills by working with the team in a project of this sort. Nevertheless, there will be parts of your job which are closed to them. You must endeavour to provide opportunities for them to gain this experience. We have already suggested ways in which this might be accomplished, by delegating tasks to them, allowing them to run and chair meetings and so on. Be alert to their needs and offer them the option of developing their skills further by working with you and becoming familiar with the nature of your job. It will be to your credit, if, when in turn your post is advertised, the people that you have trained in your team are sufficiently well qualified to be strong candidates for your job. You will know then that you have become a successful manager.

Index